JB JOSSEY-BASS™
A Wiley Brand

Online Fundraising Essentials

SECOND EDITION

Scott C. Stevenson, Editor

WILEY

For general information on our other products and services or for technical support, please contact our Customer Care Department within the United States at (800) 762-2974, outside the United States at (317) 572-3993 or fax (317) 572-4002.

Wiley publishes in a variety of print and electronic formats and by print-on-demand. Some material included with standard print versions of this book may not be included in e-books or in print-on-demand. If this book refers to media such as a CD or DVD that is not included in the version you purchased, you may download this material at http://booksupport.wiley.com. For more information about Wiley products, visit www.wiley.com.

978-1-118-67684-4   ISBN

978-1-118-70380-9   ISBN (online)

Online Fundraising Essentials
— 2nd Edition

Published by

Stevenson, Inc.

P.O. Box 4528 • Sioux City, Iowa • 51104

Phone 712.239.3010 • Fax 712.239.2166

www.stevensoninc.com

Online Fundraising Essentials, Second Edition.
Edited by Scott C. Stevenson.
© 2012 Stevenson, Inc. Published 2012 by Stevenson, Inc.

INTRODUCTION: ADDRESSING THE ESSENTIALS

The business of online giving, including ways to make your website more donor-friendly and ways to drive people to your website, is evolving into a far more advanced science these days. Whether your goal is to generate more online gifts or simply draw more attention to funding opportunities — or both — you can learn a great deal from charities across the nation who are in various stages of advancing their online fundraising efforts.

How to Integrate Fundraising Into Your Website

When developing a website, take steps to integrate your fundraising and overall strategic plan, says Michel Hudson, owner of 501(c)onsulting (Round Rock, TX).

"Your annual fundraising and major gift campaigns can all be integrated into your website as a way to get people excited about your programs," Hudson says. "One way to do that is to integrate your donor/prospect database into your online e-mail newsletter sign-up function, so that visitors who sign up for your e-newsletter are automatically added to your prospect database."

Hudson shares additional ways to integrate fundraising into your website:

- Include links throughout your electronic solicitations to direct donors and prospects to additional information on your website.

- Make sure you have consistent branding in print and online pieces so donors always know the source of information.

- Be sure to always make an ask, whether it is to respond to calls for action, become a member or donate to your programs.

- Use your website to highlight specific campaign projects or programs. For example, if you have a building project, set up a webcam and include streaming video to your website, so your constituents can see your building's progress online.

- Include an online donation form to make it easy for donors to renew their giving.

- Use your website to create volunteer and social networking opportunities. Such opportunities can lead to major gifts.

- Set up your website as an information warehouse. Use it to push information to prospects and make the information easier to access. For example, putting information online eliminates printing costs for annual reports and research reports. Online technology also provides dynamic, interesting options for delivering information.

- Show progress reports online so that donors can see where their money is going. This also makes it easy for them to see the successes your organization is having and grow more confident about supporting it.

Source: Michel Hudson, Owner, 501(c)onsulting, Round Rock, TX.
E-mail: mhudson@501consulting.com

Nonprofit Website Dos and Don'ts

Michel Hudson, owner of 501(c)onsulting (Round Rock, TX), shares steps *not* to take when developing your nonprofit website:

- ✓ Don't include a What's New box if you're not going to update it regularly. You should update a What's New box at least monthly, telling people you are keeping fresh through RSS feeds.

- ✓ Don't make members e-mail you to subscribe to your e-newsletter or other updates. Create an automatic process for joining or subscribing to those features.

- ✓ Don't refer to links that aren't active or can't be accessed.

- ✓ Don't post a thermometer or other gauge of fundraising progress until you raise at least 50 percent of your goal. If your goal is $1 million and your thermometer says you have raised $1,000, prospective donors will think your fundraising has not been successful.

Make Online Donations Easy

How easy is it to make a donation through your website?

An article by Web-usability expert Jakob Nielsen, Nielsen Norman Group, says that "on 17 percent of tested sites, website visitors couldn't even find where to go to donate."

For more info: http://www.useit.com/alertbox/nonprofit-donations.html

Tips to Make Your Website More User-friendly

Research shows that Internet users take only 10 to 20 seconds to decide whether to explore a website or leave it. Nonprofits, therefore, need to do all they can to give users what they want in the ways they want it, says Michel Hudson, chief strategist of 501 (c)onsulting (Round Rock, TX). Here, Hudson shares suggestions for critical areas of design strategy and technical approach:

Design Strategy

- Think like users. Don't use jargon, acronyms or names known only to insiders.

- Know what users are looking for — what your organization does, ways to donate, how to volunteer with you — and make it easy to find.

- Use a What's New section to keep things fresh and updated. Fresh material keeps users coming back and boosts page ranking in Google and other search engines.

- Offer information immediately. Having an entrance or splash page is just one more click standing between you and potential supporters.

- Limit the number of steps needed to take action. Says Hudson, "You don't want people having to click through 10 pages to sign up for an e-newsletter."

- Keep your domain name short, descriptive and easy to remember. Hudson suggests purchasing similar domain names if misspellings are likely to be an issue.

- Write content for users, not search engines or optimization standards.

- Keep your design clean and easy to read. Hudson suggests using Arial and Verdana — and avoiding Times New Roman — as web-friendly fonts.

- Keep content concise and scannable, using bullet points, headings and links to other pages with more information.

Tools and Techniques

- Use flash and video sparingly. "People come to your website to find information, not to be dazzled by special effects," says Hudson. She adds that some users may not have the high-speed Internet access needed for such applications.

- Use animated GIFs instead of Flash, as they have a quicker load time than Flash and support text tags, which are more effectively indexed by search engines.

- Test your site on multiple browsers before going live. Different browsers render code in significantly different ways.

- Include a title, keywords and description in every page's meta tags (part of the background coding) to optimize search engine ranking. Metadata must reflect page content, though, cautions Hudson. For example, a key word will not be highly ranked by Google unless it appears at least three times on a page.

- Use website analytics such as Google Analytics (www.google.com/analytics) to track how your website is accessed and used.

- Integrate website data-gathering with operations such as member or donor databases to avoid duplicate shadow databases.

Source: Michel Hudson, Chief Strategist, 501(c)onsulting, Round Rock, TX. E-mail: mhudson@501consulting.com.

Checklist Cites Must-have Website Features

No matter what your mission, you can make your website more accessible and user-friendly, says Michel Hudson, chief strategist of 501 (c)onsulting (Round Rock, TX). To do so, she advises, be sure your website includes:

- ❑ **A privacy/security statement.** "This makes people feel more inclined to make a donation or share their personal information," says Hudson.

- ❑ **Contact information,** including physical address, e-mail, phone and fax number on every page. Hudson suggests including a copyright year to show information is current.

- ❑ **An About Us page.** Hudson says that while content on the home page will overlap somewhat, a dedicated About Us page is still necessary.

- ❑ **A mechanism to donate/join/etc. on every page.** "Having a call to action on every page ensures that users, no matter where they are or what they are doing, can take that next step," she says.

- ❑ **An organizational tagline that defines your organization and what it does.** Examples include, "Explore, enjoy and protect the planet," (The Sierra Club) and "Where volunteering begins" (Volunteer Match).

- ❑ **A search function or site map** to help people connect with information or resources they seek.

- ❑ **Polls, surveys or raffles.** These reinforce connections with your organization and get people coming back to your website.

- ❑ **Free resources** such as downloadable articles, papers, stories or forms, that position your organization as a provider of professional value.

Web Presence Especially Important for Little-known Causes

Little-known causes almost always face an uphill battle when it comes to name awareness. And while the Internet is perhaps the world's most expansive communication tool, it's also a place where your nonprofit organization is competing for attention alongside an infinite number of websites, news sources and other online distractions.

If most people don't know what your nonprofit is or what it does, how do you create ways to draw online traffic?

One such organization that is meeting this challenge is Jacob's Cure (www.jacobscure.org) of Rye, NY, a nonprofit dedicated to raising funds to find a cure for Canavan Disease, a fatal genetic disorder that is diagnosed in about 200 children every year. Officials at the nonprofit have developed a number of techniques to get its message out online, with results that can be seen offline, as well. For example, in recent years Jacob's Cure has organized an event at the Library of Congress hosted by Hillary Clinton.

"Not every person you talk to will become an advocate for your brand," says Sarah Goshman, assistant director of Jacob's Cure, "but a lot of people will because you've created a personal connection with them."

Here are key parts of Jacob's Cure's online awareness-raising strategies:

✓ **Make use of free advertising for nonprofits.** Many social media platforms and big-name websites offer some sort of discounted or free services to nonprofit users. Says Goshman, "We are the recipient of a Google Grant and receive free Adwords advertising courtesy of Google. We have a nonprofit account with YouTube. We also make use of Facebook ads to reach people who are already connected to our network, but not directly to us."

✓ **Start a blog.** Fold it into your already-existing website or link to it prominently from your website. Jacob's Cure started a blog about a year ago, Goshman says, "which has brought in a lot of traffic and made us more searchable because we try to write on different topics." Another bonus a blog can bring: By featuring guest bloggers — those with some sort of link to your cause, such as prominent researchers, established authors, etc. — you create opportunities to establish relationships with all of your guest bloggers' connections.

✓ **Target your tweets effectively.** On Twitter, "I try to interact with people who are talking about topics relevant to what we do," says Goshman, "and I have connected us with a number of women in the mom-blog community as well as on special-needs blogs and forums."

Source: Sarah Goshman, Assistant Director, Jacob's Cure, Rye, NY.
E-mail: sarah@jacobscure.org.

Dos and Don'ts When Crafting Specific Calls to Action

Sarah Goshman, assistant director of the nonprofit, Jacob's Cure (Rye, NY), shares what to do — and what not to do — in crafting calls to action via social media and other electronic methods:

- **Don't just ask people to do something.** When Jacob's Cure was participating in the Pepsi Refresh campaign, which awards grant money to nonprofit causes that receive the most online votes, "we were posting every day asking people to vote and not really seeing any response on our Facebook page," Goshman says.

- **Do use the 'Like' function on Facebook.** Says Goshman, "One day we posted, 'Like this status if you voted today!' and over 60 people responded in a few hours."

- **Do ask people to donate or take some action on behalf of one child (or personalize your mission, in terms of the impact it has on one person).** "This tends to get more significant results than when we talk about saving all the Canavan children worldwide," says Goshman. "People like to read someone else's story — it makes the cause much more personal to them."

Don't Overlook Online Giving

Think online giving is only for small donations or annual funding needs? Think again.

The Blackbaud Online Giving Report (http://www.blackbaud.com/bb/online/fundraising.aspx) shows 88 percent of organizations received at least one online gift of $1,000 or more. And while the median online gift of $1,000 or more was a relatively modest $1,250, the largest was a full $100,000.

What does this mean for your organization? As online giving grows increasingly widespread, it will become critical to avoid unintentionally inclining online donors toward smaller gifts. Be sure digital interfaces, solicitation communications and staff attitudes welcome major online gifts.

Online Giving Tip

■ To bring back visitors to your website repeatedly (and hopefully encourage multiple gifts), vary your site's content with fresh news and photos. A content management system (CMS) allows non-programmers to regularly upload new text and photos.

Know Which Social Media Site Is Right for Your Organization

With the proliferation of social media, most every organization is looking to jump on board. But should you Tweet or update your news feed? And where does LinkedIn fit in?

Michael Howard, principal of At Your Service Business Consulting (Albany, NY), helps nonprofits answer these and other questions as they build their Web and social media presence. He recently helped the local chapter of a national organization nearly triple attendance at an annual event through Facebook.

Here, Howard shares quick guidelines to determine how to use social media to benefit your cause:

- Facebook is about long-term engagement with supporters who want to have fun volunteering and supporting the organization.
- Twitter is important when the organization is involved in lobbying for legislative changes and has a lot going on that lends itself to short, immediate messages with no shelf life.
- LinkedIn is great for membership organizations that want to create discussion groups with their membership, improve programming and help members professionally.
- Blogs are great for organizations that want to bring a more personal face to what they do, especially if it is in a difficult-to-understand academic or scientific field.

Source: Michael Howard, Principal, At Your Service Business Consulting, Albany, NY. Phone (518) 449-2420. E-mail: mhoward@consider-done.com. Website: www.consider-done.com

Facebook Can Help Your Event

In addition to boosting attendance at your next event, Michael Howard, principal, At Your Service Business Consulting (Albany, NY) says Facebook can help you:

1. **Recognize sponsors.** When a company decides to donate, post that information on your page.
2. **Create a sense of urgency.** Post items such as, "Over 500 tickets have been purchased — Don't miss out!" or "Last day for advance ticket sales."
3. **Attract different demographics.** For example, this medium can help the very desirable 25-40 demographic realize that for very little investment, they can become philanthropists. It also presents a stewardship opportunity, because they may become more involved in the organization's committees and other events.

Multilingualism Online: Know Your Community

Many nonprofit organizations serve individuals for whom English is not a primary language. Some organizations offer multilingual services in phone systems and print literature but may omit the service online or in development literature. This oversight is potentially damaging to your cause; as any development officer knows, the more people who benefit from your service, the more attractive your organization will be to potential donors.

Make sure your development staff knows the cultural demographics of the community they are serving, and can point to multilingual or translation services within your organization. While foreign-language speakers may not currently be among your intended donor population, they might have a connection to someone who is.

Furthermore, stepping up to get your message out to all members of your service area — not just those who happen to speak English — will illustrate the extra length your organization is willing to go to connect to your community. This could attract potential donors to your cause, as such sensitivity adds yet another link in that vital connection between a donor and the recipient of that donor's generosity.

Add Personal Touches to Online Media Kits

Online or multimedia press kits can be a boon to nonprofit organizations that want to sell and tell their stories not just through numbers and statistics, but through human interest.

Says Jules Zunich, president of Z Group PR (www.zgrouppr.com) of Boise, ID, which works extensively with nonprofits, "What makes a great story is not necessarily the work that the nonprofit is doing, but the people it has helped."

Your online media kit should provide access not just to your organization's experts, but to clients of yours with success stories to share. "A journalist may not want to interview an expert. They often want to speak to the people whose lives have been affected," says Zunich. It's not enough to just allude on your website to being able to put reporters in touch with such people: "Having those stories in an easily accessed format is vital."

Consider adding links to videos and written, first-person accounts. (These can be written by a client, or a communications staffer can interview a client and write up a Q&A for the kit.) Zunich also recommends including a case study or two, as they do a good job of "connecting the dots" between a nonprofit's work and the personal effects that work has on everyday people.

Source: Jules Zunich, President, Z Group PR, Boise, ID. E-mail: julia@zgrouppr.com

Online Fundraising Essentials, Second Edition.
Edited by Scott C. Stevenson.
© 2012 Stevenson, Inc. Published 2012 by Stevenson, Inc.

Online Fundraising Essentials — 2ⁿᵈ Edition

BUILD YOUR LIST AND ENGAGE WEBSITE VISITORS

Raising funds online starts with building your website community: capturing e-mail addresses, driving more people to your website, engaging them and more. Making your website into an effective fundraising and donor cultivation tool requires a variety of strategies aimed at attracting, involving and accommodating both donors and would-be donors. It's one thing to attract people to your site; it's another to keep them coming back for more.

Drive Potential Donors to Your Website

Your organization's website features valuable information, as well as an easy and secure online donation process. But what good is the site without traffic?

Here are six ways to drive potential donors to your organization's website:

1. **Encourage referrals.** Include a refer-a-friend option on your website that lets visitors send an e-mail to friends suggesting they check out your website. (We all know a friend's suggestion truly means something!) Consider the same option for your e-newsletter.

2. **Be a tease.** If your organization does not have a blog, start one. Blogs are a great way to share your message. To get people to visit your site, entice them with a teaser. For instance, if your website features informational articles, post the first few lines on your blog, along with a link to your website to read the rest of the story.

3. **YouTube.** Ask a local college to help make a short video or develop a video campaign to post on YouTube. Be sure to check out YouTube's nonprofit program (www.youtube.com/nonprofits) and create your own channel. When making the video, mention or show your organization's web address several times.

4. **Offer incentives.** Give people a reason to visit your site. For instance, encourage persons to register for a drawing. Or, pose a question in your newsletter with directions to visit your website for the answer.

5. **Trade links.** Ask other nonprofit organizations or event sponsors to include a link to your website from theirs. Don't forget to ask that CEO on your board of directors to post a link on his/her company site.

6. **Apply for a Google Grant** (www.google.com/grants). Recipients receive at least three months of free advertising up to $10,000 per month. As a recipient, you'll choose keywords relevant to your organization. When Google users search for those keywords, your AdWords ad will appear. Users can click on the ad and go directly to your website.

Seventeen Ways to Capture E-mail Addresses

Reasons to collect e-mail addresses — making connections, building relationships, developing leads, promoting products, soliciting feedback, recruiting new members, to name a few — are obvious. Practical ways to collect them are not always as clear.

Here are 17 methods to help build and expand your e-mail contact list.

1. Include a sign-up to your e-mail list on every page of your website.
2. Offer discounts/incentives to members who refer friends to your materials.
3. Use social media services such as Facebook and Twitter to direct contacts to a landing page or sign-up form.
4. Hold a contest (blogging, photography, etc.) that communicates announcements, updates and winners by e-mail.
5. Advertise e-mail-only coupons or discounts on your website.
6. Update databases by calling or sending a postcard to bounce-back contacts.
7. Put an offer for your newsletter (or other online service) on the back of your business card.
8. Bring a clipboard to trade shows and conventions to capture addresses of those interested in knowing more about your organization.
9. Make high-interest white papers, articles or reports available online in return for a valid e-mail address.
10. Include a newsletter sign-up link in the signature line of all your e-mails.
11. Send postal-only contacts a special offer to join your e-mail list.
12. Trade newsletter space and links to e-mail opt-in forms with an organization in your industry area.
13. Make supplying a valid e-mail address part of registering for a webinar, virtual speaker or podcast.
14. Offer free e-courses — groups of four to seven articles concerning the same topic — to anyone interested in receiving them via e-mail.
15. Use a pop-up window to ask for e-mail addresses when persons attempt to leave your website (or certain pages).
16. Add an opt-in form to your Facebook page, so visitors can sign up on the spot.
17. Instruct front-line personnel to conclude phone conversations by asking for the person's current e-mail address.

What Donors Expect From Your Website

Donors have certain expectations when visiting your website, says Michel Hudson, owner of 501(c)onsulting (Round Rock, TX): "Donors want to feel connected to your organization and as though they are part of your family. They also want to know that you have similar outlooks and objectives to theirs."

To fulfill those donor expectations, says Hudson:

- **Have compelling website copy.** Your text needs to compel them to donate, participate in a call to action and/or read more about your organization. It should inform people about your cause, what you are doing and how they can help.

- **Tell them where the money goes.** This makes them feel confident about your cause.

- **Share your research and any results, insights or successes.** People want to know more about what interests them and that's why they are coming to your site.

- **Make it easy and secure for visitors to make donations.** You want to limit the number of steps it takes to get to the donation.

- **Include a prominent and well-stated privacy policy.**

- **Make sure website content is fresh.** This gives donors confidence in your organization. "Be aware that search engine optimization is based on freshness," Hudson notes. "The more your content changes, the higher rankings you will get with search engines. But don't change things just for change — make it meaningful."

Source: Michel Hudson, Owner, 501(c)onsulting, Round Rock, TX. E-mail: mhudson@501consulting.com

Create Podcasts That Draw Attention and Interest

Podcasts are an effective way to train staff or volunteers, send a message to members, educate constituents and inform the public about your organization. Podcasts allow users to view visual and audio components from your website or by links sent directly to them.

Getting your message across cleanly and professionally is critical. Make your podcasts shine by:

- **Preparing in advance for interviews.** If you are interviewing a subject, prepare a good number of interview questions prior to recording your podcast. In addition to a list of initial questions, be sure to have follow-up questions ready to help clarify content.

- **Preparing the interviewee.** Prepare your interviewees by providing them with a sampling of questions they'll be expected to answer. This will allow them to formulate relevant and thorough answers.

- **Including links.** When posting your podcast on your website, be sure to include links to any presentation materials or corresponding information to assist the viewer in obtaining all information on the topic presented.

- **Working with an editor.** Consider hiring or finding someone familiar with podcast editing to polish your appeal or training recording. If you're planning on offering frequent podcasts, an experienced editor will add production value to your presentations and consistency to your communications, which will increase viewership.

- **Offering a written transcript of your podcasts.** Offer written transcripts to promote a broader use of your materials and better access for all who wish to utilize the information.

Online Toolkit Strengthens Affinity Groups

With 18 affinity groups and counting, the Georgia Tech Alumni Association (Atlanta, GA) knows more than a little about keeping members involved and engaged. And for the past seven years, the association has relied on an online toolkit to help groups be as effective as possible.

"The toolkit was created to help groups get established and be sustainable and successful," says Debra Thompson, senior manager of affinity groups. "It's also packed with information that they can continue to refer back to for guidance and assistance."

The toolkit, which can be found at http://gtalumni.org/pages/affinitygrouptoolkit, contains template-style resources like officer update forms, financial year-end report forms and event recording forms. It also offers more general guidelines and best practices gathered from successful groups.

For organizations putting together a similar toolkit, Thompson says to focus first on a clearly defined mission — for both the institution and the group itself — and then develop practical guidelines that will keep a group within the bounds of that mission.

She also says personal communication and interaction is crucial — she characterizes the meetings and training sessions she has with groups as "an extension of the toolkit itself" and a major component of what allows groups to be successful in the long run.

Source: Debra Thompson, Senior Manager, Affinity Groups, Georgia Tech Alumni Association, Atlanta, GA. E-mail: Debra.thompson@alumni.gatech.edu

Vary Content to Attract Blog Audience

Few magazines feature nothing but text; they build interest with features, illustrations and photo spreads. Doing the same thing with your blog will draw attention and incline readers to return to your content again and again.

✓ **Update at regular intervals.** Determine at the outset when to publish new materials, whether it be daily or once or twice a week. A disciplined approach helps readers determine how often to check in and comment. If there's nothing new for days or weeks, they may stop looking.

✓ **Engage readers with photos, polls and links.** Support or supplement your news and opinions with content that gives readers additional information, a chance to debate or exclusive announcements.

✓ **Relentlessly edit posts.** Make every word count, so readers know they get maximum information with a minimum amount of time. Remember that many read blogs on smart phones and other hand-held devices with tiny screens.

✓ **Respond to reader comments.** Your blog readers leave comments — sometimes praise, sometimes criticism — and probably check back to see if you have replied. Keep up with as many as possible, using replies as a chance to provide additional information, to thank them for making a point and to encourage lurkers to become engaged as well.

✓ **Know when to move on to new topics.** The more comments a post generates, the more tempting it is to keep the ball rolling by responding even if only to the same few people. Have plenty of other topics for readers who are no longer interested in that discussion.

✓ **Use your blog to recognize and thank people.** Mention by name as many readers, supporters and volunteers as you can. Encourage other readers to add their positive comments. Some who normally don't participate will add their remarks when given a chance to offer praise. You may also discover followers you didn't know you had, which helps you further tailor content to your audience.

List Management Tips

■ Do all of your printed materials ask for an e-mail address? E-mail offers an ever-growing medium for notifying, cultivating and, in some instances, soliciting constituents.

Invite Bounce Backs on Your Website

The reasons for inviting website visitors to provide you with input are many. Doing so engages them in the work of your organization; it requires that they share their e-mail addresses; and their ideas and opinions may provide you with valuable insight.

Here are a few examples of prompts you may want to include or tailor to fit your organization:

- The first 50 people to send in correct answers to the following questions will receive a gift.

- Do you know the answers to these trivia questions about (name of organization)?

- We're looking for examples of.... If you can help, please reply.

- We're taking a vote on this important issue. Please share your response.

- Do you have news to share for the next issue of our newsletter? Click here to share it with us.

Increase Board Productivity With A Dedicated Intranet

To increase the efficiency and effectiveness of board members, staff and volunteers, streamline information and resource sharing with a dedicated organizational intranet.

The intranet at the San Diego Asian Film Foundation (www.sdaff.org), San Diego, CA, "is a private online space where stakeholders can find everything from time cards to information on current and prospective grants," says Lee Ann Kim, executive director.

Using unique user names and passwords, board members use the intranet to find staff contact information, detailed biographies of other board members, meeting schedules, calendars and key financial information, along with connecting board membership with sponsorship records.

"Savvy fundraisers can click on any of the 500 or so sponsors that have supported us over the last 12 years and see their history of giving, any recent interactions with us, and a current name and contact number," says Kim. "They never have to wonder if this or that company is on board with a project."

She says the system, custom built for the foundation in 2002, was revolutionary for its time. While it still offers many advantages, Kim says applications like Googledocs have come to approximate many of its functions.

Source: Lee Ann Kim, Executive Director, San Diego Asian Film Foundation, San Diego, CA. E-mail: Leeann@sdaff.org.

Online Fundraising Essentials, Second Edition.
Edited by Scott C. Stevenson.
© 2012 Stevenson, Inc. Published 2012 by Stevenson, Inc.

MAKE YOUR WEBSITE PERSONAL, INTERACTIVE

To draw people in to your website's content, make their experiences more personal and more interactive. Emerging technologies are enabling this in an ever-growing number of ways: social networking (Facebook, Twitter, LinkedIn), mini-websites, personalized websites, members-only portals, affinity groups and more.

Social Networking as a Fundraising Tool: Myths vs. Realities

To innovate its approach to fundraising, St. Olaf College (www.stolaf.edu/giving) of Northfield, MN, has joined the universe of social networking. St. Olaf can be found on Twitter, Facebook, Myspace and LinkedIn. In addition, St. Olaf reunion volunteers have created class-specific groups and fan pages to promote their reunions.

Matt Fedde, associate director of annual giving, answers questions on what social networking means for higher education fundraising:

Why did you decide to try social networking as a fundraising tool?

"We thought, 'All good online social networking is free, so why not?' The decision to get involved was easy and so was creating the accounts. The tricky part now is trying to figure out how to create quality content for these accounts and to figure out how our presence on these sites can translate into increased gifts to the annual fund."

After gaining friends/fans/contacts, what kind of maintenance does the site require?

"The only social networking service I've been really excited about is Twitter. So it's the one that I've really put energy into in terms of content and reaching out to fans/followers. I look each follower up in our alumni database — if there's a match I send a hello message, welcoming them to give me suggestions for improvements. There is good potential for growth with this — we could do Tweet-ups or target e-mail messages or any number of different targeted messages or events. The nice thing is there's no fee to have an account on any of these sites and we don't pay someone to create content. Most tweets are auto-generated from official college RSS feeds. Depending on my workload, I may spend zero to three hours a week on maintaining the accounts.

"We are considering implementing personal fundraising sites. They were very successful with the Obama campaign, and I've seen them for friends running marathons. But because the cost to implement them is fairly high, and there is some uncertainty that the success they have in irregular, deadline-oriented fundraising projects will be able to translate to giving annually to an educational institution."

What kind of response has your office seen to their social networking efforts?

"One challenge has been to quantify the response we've had. There's no real way to know if our presence on these sites results in increased giving.... Our official annual giving Facebook account has 20 fans. The official St. Olaf Alumni Facebook group has about 2,500 members.... An unofficial, renegade and fairly inactive Facebook St. Olaf College fan page has 3,000 fans. By contrast, our MySpace had 37 views in the past year. Then, our alumni LinkedIn group has 2,250 members. Our Twitter has 500 followers (20 to 30 of whom are traceable alumni) and each tweet link gets four to 35 clicks.

"In terms of Facebook fundraising, an attempt to raise money via Facebook cause bore only $35 in revenue. But when comparing FY '08 to FY '09, we saw a 60 percent increase in the number of online gifts and a 38 percent increase in amount raised through our gift site. Our social networking presence could have contributed to this, but if I were to guess, I'd say that it's more of a national trend than a result of our hard e-work."

What are your other fundraising efforts and their relative success? Which are innovative or new for St. Olaf? How are social networking efforts similar/dissimilar to these?

"Within annual giving, our primary programs are volunteer (reunion and non-reunion), direct mail, e-mail, phoning and the Senior Class Campaign.... Our primary work has been to shift focus from institutional fundraising (solicitation that comes from the college as direct mail or e-mail) to peer-to-peer volunteer fundraising (classmate-to-classmate e-mail, phone calls, letters, etc). We've seen great success with this in a handful of classes, and are working to replicate their success across all graduated classes. Social networking sites may eventually help with this, but we have yet to figure out exactly how."

Source: Matthew Fedde, Associate Director of Annual Giving, St. Olaf College, Northfield, MN.

> ### Check Out Social Network Sites
>
> ✓ Myspace (www.myspace.com/ucsantabarbara)
>
> ✓ Twitter (www.twitter.com/macalester)

Draw Attention, Pique Interest With Personalized Websites

Everyone knows a letter addressed to John and Mary Jones will evoke far more response than one addressed to Valued Supporters. That kind of familiarity once reserved for mail-merge documents is now available online with personalized URLs.

"A personalized URL is basically a website whose content is tailored to a specific individual or family," says Joseph Hoag, former director of stewardship and development at the Roman Catholic Diocese of Erie, PA, which won an award from the Direct Marketing Association (New York, NY) for an innovative direct mail campaign utilizing personalized URLs.

The campaign focused on three oversized postcards, sent to lapsed donors at three- to four-week intervals, asking, "What does it mean to be Catholic?" The back of each mailing offered a short answer such as, "It means I belong," and a personalized web address incorporating the donor's name.

Persons visiting the URL found a website personalized with information such as links to the visitor's home parish, information about that congregation's activities or a picture of the priest the visitor would find at his or her parish.

Sent to donors who had not contributed in at least four years, the mailer achieved a response rate (recipients visiting their website) of over 8 percent. Even more impressive was its impact on fundraising. Though the campaign was considered a form of pastoral outreach and solicitation was scrupulously avoided, a diocesan-wide appeal following the final mailing elicited contributions from 14 percent of recipients, raising over $120,000.

Hoag says personalized URLs work best in volume and in situations where attention is caught by a succession of messages featuring the same website. They can also be used for purposes such as in-depth information gathering or to cater messages or imagery to certain demographics.

The campaign cost $12,500 ($10,000 for third-party programming and $2,500 for production/postage) and was developed and implemented in collaboration with the Cathedral Corporation of Rome, NY, which was a co-recipient of the Direct Marketing Association award.

Source: Joseph Hoag, National Account Manager for Diocesan Solutions, Cathedral Corporation, Rome, NY.
E-mail: Jhoag@cathedralcorporation.com

Personal Websites Bring Smiles to Donors, Children in Need

The more closely a person relates to an organization's mission, the more motivated he or she is to donate money to it and ask others to donate, too.

C. Eric Overman, director of online and interactive, Operation Smile (Norfolk, VA), says its OneSmile program definitely makes their mission real and relatable for those donors who use it. OneSmile allows donors to easily set up their own Web page to raise funds to cover the cost of life-changing surgery for one child.

The ability to make a personal page provided the perfect way to connect supporters to the cause online, Overman says.

"In a few easy steps, online donors can build their own Web page, tell their story and invite friends to join in. Just like with social media, it is a friend asking you to support us, not us asking you for money," he says, adding, "Since we launched (the personal page option in 2007), almost 400 pages have been set up, raising nearly $150,000."

When considering such a project, Overman says to make sure you have the technology necessary to run the program and that the technology fully integrates into your other systems.

Also, he says, be aware of the costs, which can vary greatly depending on several factors, including your current Web and e-mail platforms and in-house technology resources.

Finally, have a plan to market the opportunity to current and prospective donors.

"Just because you build it doesn't mean they will come," he says. "You will still need to promote the site and integrate custom campaigns into the major events and marketing campaigns running across your organization."

Source: C. Eric Overman, Director of Online and Interactive, Operation Smile, Norfolk, VA.
E-mail: eoverman@operationsmile.org

Engage Website Visitors

- **Take periodic polls.** Asking visitors for their opinion on a specific topic serves as a great way to engage them. Plus, you may learn something from their collective responses. Polldaddy (www.polldaddy.com) is one free tool you can use to create surveys and polls for your website.

Mini-websites Help Raise Funds for Nonprofit's Mission

If your organization's membership and fundraising staff are stretched thin or you are simply looking for a way to engage members, consider sharing important duties with your supporters by creating a program that lets them take an active role in raising funds for your mission.

After years of donor-led fundraising events (e.g., birthday parties, weddings, special events, etc.) staff with the World Wildlife Fund (WWF) of Washington, D.C., decided a change was needed, and launched Panda Pages in summer 2008.

Panda Pages is a section on WWF's website where persons create their own mini-websites to help raise money, raise awareness for the organization or a particular issue and connect with family and friends.

"The process of the fundraising events was cumbersome for donors and time-intensive for staff to manage," says David Glass, director, online marketing. "Our donors had to do much of the outreach, communication, fundraising and operations on their own. And, the entire effort was off-line, which made it challenging for a donor to gather and consolidate donations.

"It was time to give the donor much more control by putting the fundraising tools into the hands of our energetic and passionate supporters," he says.

Now by visiting the Panda Pages section (www.worldwildlife.org/mypanda) on WWF's website, supporters can customize a page in support of the organization's mission in about 10 minutes. The page can be customized to mark a special occasion, honor a friend or loved one, or simply highlight their passion for protecting endangered species.

The mini-websites allow supporters to:

✓ Send e-mails to friends and family asking them to visit the page;
✓ Raise money to help support WWF's conservation work;
✓ Connect with members who are passionate about wildlife conservation;
✓ Upload and share photos of favorite animals and nature places; and
✓ Help protect endangered species and places around the world.

Glass says supporters have two options when creating a page: public and private. A public page can be viewed or used by anyone who comes across the site, while only those who are specially invited may see a private page. Glass says near the holidays many families use the private pages to share information related to conservation and wildlife, conduct private fundraising, and share gift giving and donations online.

Source: David Glass, Director, Online Marketing, World Wildlife Fund, Washington, D.C. E-mail: David.glass@wwfus.org

---

Factors to Consider With User-based Fundraising Tool

A user-based fundraising tool like Panda Pages has several appealing benefits, says David Glass, director, online marketing, World Wildlife Fund (Washington, D.C.).

Those benefits include:

1. Donors and friends get a convenient, easy-to-use and efficient way to support their favorite cause.

2. The nonprofit gets an economical and efficient way to connect with many donors at a time for event-, theme- or topic-based fundraising.

Glass also shares two issues that are important to acknowledge with a new tool like this:

1. Putting more control in the hands of your organization's friends and donors means expecting and accepting that the messaging and language they use will vary and most likely be as "on message" as the language used by the organization to promote its own issues.

2. It's useful to train a customer service team to help with any questions or concerns a donor may have.

A More Advanced Approach to Locating Lost Alumni

As important a donor pool as alumni are, reconnecting with them would seem to be a major priority for schools and universities. Yet most lost-alumni Web pages offer little more than a list of names and a university e-mail address or phone number to contact with more information about lost alumni.

Brandeis University (Waltham, MA) bucks this trend. The interactive interface on its lost alumni Web page (http://alumni.brandeis.edu/web/classes/lost_alumni.html) lets users search for undergraduates by class year, graduates by school and sorted by class year or last name, and scholarship recipients by class year.

This level of user interaction allows more streamlined data gathering, says Brian Dowling, principal of SupportingAdvancement.com (Vancouver, British Columbia, Canada) and a seasoned consultant on issues of data and records management. Dowling says clicking the link on any name leads to a multi-field input form, personalized to the graduate in question, which facilitates integration with the university's primary alumni database.

Source: Brian Dowling, Principal, SupportingAdvancement.com, Vancouver, British Columbia, Canada. E-mail: brian.dowling@supportingadvancement.com

Create Feel of Real-life Giving With Online Tools

Nadanu Technologies (Brooklyn, NY) has launched www.Nadanu.com, a website that offers eOfferingPlate, CampaignRaiser and eCharityBox, online tools that mimic real-life giving to provide donors with interactive experiences such as dropping coins into a box or onto an offering plate.

CEO Getzy Fellig says that eOfferingPlate (geared toward religious organizations) and eCharityBox (broader in scope) are the two more popular product lines. Rates for these services begin at $19.95 per month, plus a percentage of each transaction. The tools include the interactive giving mechanism on an organization's website, a branded Facebook app, an iPhone app and branded website designed for mobile phones.

"Some organizations don't have the staff or knowledge for how to be properly positioned in the ever-growing list of technology platforms, social media and the Internet," Fellig says. "Nadanu's products are turnkey. There is absolutely nothing for them to do other than inform their donors that the program exists."

Nadanu also e-mails automated tax receipts to donors and provides a financial report to the nonprofit. An organization can use Nadanu's technology to distribute content to its donors and members; for example, if a client loads a video onto its Nadanu platform, that video will automatically appear on every social media interface (website, Facebook, etc.) that the nonprofit has hooked up with Nadanu's technology.

More than 500 nonprofit organizations currently use at least one of Nadanu's three product lines, says Fellig, noting that The Salvation Army has worked with Nadanu on custom design work to recreate the feeling of giving online to its iconic Christmas kettle.

Dena Schusterman, director of Intown Jewish Preschool (www.intownjewishpreschool.org) of Atlanta, GA, is a Nadanu client who found out about the company via an e-mail blast. "We had hoped to bring in the small donor on a more ongoing basis, as well as to bring a convenience to giving via mobile applications, and in general, to create an easier avenue for giving," Schusterman says. "I've been very satisfied. I think Nadanu's services are well-suited to any organization of any size that wishes to be present in the era of technology we are in now."

Sources: Getzy Fellig, CEO Nadanu Technologies, Brooklyn, NY. E-mail: gfellig@nadanu.com.
Dena Schusterman, Director, Intown Jewish Preschool, Atlanta, GA. E-mail: dena@chabadintown.org.

Custom Facebook Pages Boost Event Attendance

Imagine if you could triple attendance at one of your organization's long-standing events. Technology and social media can help make that happen, says Michael Howard, principal, At Your Service Business Consulting (Albany, NY).

Howard says he helped the local chapter of the Leukemia and Lymphoma Society (LLS) use Facebook to increase attendance at its annual Taste of Compassion wine-tasting event from an average of 250 attendees to nearly 650 over two years.

To do so, Howard designed an expanded mini-website page, known as a custom Facebook page, which allowed more photos and copy, PDF downloads and links to buy tickets.

The Taste of Compassion Facebook page brought people involved with other parts of the organization, such as 1,200 persons involved in a marathon fundraising program, in as fans. Howard says Facebook opened up a huge communications medium with those people — most of whom are younger — about how "cool" the wine tasting event is.

Regular updates on prizes, wineries and ticket sales had a viral effect, leading sponsors and friends of sponsors to become fans.

He says the first year using Facebook saw attendance grow from 250 to 400, necessitating a change in venue. The following year, the event drew 650.

Howard says the custom page also serves as a cross-promotion platform for events throughout the year.

"Fans rarely leave, so it is easy to place a post on the Taste of Compassion page for their spring event, which also has its own Facebook page," he says.

"The LLS chapter has its own page for communication not related to a particular event. All of the organization's pages keep them in communication with their most likely supporters, creating a community around supporters of the organization and allowing them to communicate with each other. This can't be achieved with traditional fundraising mailings and telemarketing campaigns."

Source: Michael Howard, Principal, At Your Service Business Consulting, Albany, NY. E-mail: mhoward@consider-done.com.

Online Fundraising Essentials, Second Edition.
Edited by Scott C. Stevenson.
© 2012 Stevenson, Inc. Published 2012 by Stevenson, Inc.

Online Fundraising Essentials — 2ⁿᵈ Edition

Whether building a base of Facebook fans, tweeting announcements, distributing an e-newsletter, publishing a blog or sharing events through a podcast, nonprofits have more avenues of communication than ever to establish, cultivate and steward relationships with donors and probable donors. These communications methods can be invaluable in broadening and deepening relationships with your organization.

Look to Social Media to Expand Your Fundraising Reach

Social media is one of the trendiest ways nonprofits can raise funds. But with your budget and staff already stretched, how can you implement social media into your efforts?

Take a cue from Big Brothers Big Sisters of America (BBBS), a Philadelphia, PA-based nonprofit that uses many social media venues. Here, Cheyenne Palma, director of development, shares what works for the organization:

Twitter (www.twitter.com) is one of the largest online social networking sites and it's easy to get lost in all the tweets. How do you use this site productively?

"We try to tweet once a day during the work week, and we only follow legitimate people who follow us (trying to avoid the spammers). We also follow up with a direct message to further engage new followers."

Facebook (www.facebook.com) is another site that is seeing exponential growth. How does your Facebook fan page work for you?

"We have 4,035 fans, an increase of more than 40 percent for the year and our Facebook Causes site (a part of Facebook that allows 501(c)3 organizations to receive donations through Facebook) currently has 1,896 members who have donated $613. To keep the fan page current and reduce time spent on it, we simply integrated our RSS feed into the site. We've also learned much of our current donor base is active on Facebook and through research and data analysis, we have located nearly 20 percent of them on the site. We've recently formalized our efforts to invite them to connect with us on Facebook."

LinkedIn (www.linkedin.com) is known more for its corporate network and as a place for like-minded business people to connect. Do you feel nonprofit fundraising has a place on LinkedIn?

"We are still in the very early stages of determining how we will use LinkedIn. We've begun to identify board members and donors who are active on LinkedIn, but have yet to complete this analysis. We have discussed using the Events module and the Groups functionality to connect with specific donors and supporters on LinkedIn. We anticipate this will be a much more targeted effort and not as broad an approach as Facebook."

It seems that cell phones can do just about everything now, including depositing paychecks online. Will BBBS dip its toes in the mobile giving waters?

"We are now piloting the ability to donate funds via texting and we have 11 agencies testing text giving. Primarily, we are testing its usage at local events, such as radiothons and baseball games. It appears there is potential where we have a very large, captive audience. Our East Tennessee affiliate received 83 donations in response to a recent radiothon in their market.

"We also anticipate folding mobile giving into our social media fundraising efforts through fundraising widgets. By placing a text-giving widget on select sites, viewers won't even need to go to a separate donation page to contribute; they can simply send a text."

What do you think is important for non-profits venturing into social media to remember? And if they're not already doing it, should they be?

"It's very important for nonprofits to be involved in social media, particularly because it's the wave of the future. If you look at future generations of donors, it's how they communicate.

"An exaggerated example of this was demonstrated in a news article I read online recently about two teenage girls in Australia trapped in a storm drain — they updated their Facebook status instead of dialing for help! This is the future donor base that fundraisers are looking at tapping into; they need to get on board now, even if it's just to get their name and their message out there.

"Even from a budgetary perspective it makes sense: a few personnel hours per week can lead to donations that you might not otherwise have gotten, and there's no outside overhead to set it up or maintain it, if you do it all in-house."

Source: Cheyenne Palma, Director of Development, Big Brothers Big Sisters, Philadelphia, PA. E-mail: cheyenne.palma@bbbs.org

Reach Out to Audiences With Simple Electronic Newsletter

An electronic newsletter, or e-newsletter, could be the best communications tool in your toolbox for raising awareness about your organization while attracting media coverage, volunteers and financial support.

One of the most compelling reasons for considering this online method of connecting with your audiences is that it need not be overcomplicated. A simple, clean masthead with your organization's name, logo and contact information can be followed with whatever information you wish to communicate.

That's the design and method behind the e-newsletter for The Loft Literary Center (www.loft.org) of Minneapolis, MN. Designed to reach out to volunteers, the e-newsletter quickly informs recipients of volunteer opportunities at upcoming events, says Dara Syrkin, associate communications director/ volunteer coordinator.

The nonprofit center staff use the e-mail marketing service, Constant Contact (www. constantcontact.com), to distribute the electronic newsletter to persons in their volunteer database. Using this venue, Syrkin says, helps them to quickly and efficiently engage nearly 200 volunteers to serve audience members and artists at literary events.

"The volunteer e-newsletter is great, because I reach 550 people quickly and inexpensively," Syrkin says. "I know how effective it is because of the speed at which people respond. The Loft's volunteers are amazing! And, if by chance I don't have enough help for a certain event, I send out a plea and people always respond."

A volunteer e-newsletter can be a call to fill volunteer spaces, a reminder to committed volunteers or a medium for offering more information to volunteers.

Add details to your volunteer e-newsletter to communicate most effectively, Syrkin advises, and shares tips for accomplishing this:

- Don't be afraid to include some volunteer need-to-know information, such as designated arrival time, what to wear and what to expect. For example, add reminders at the top, bottom or side such as: "Friendly reminder: Your volunteer shift begins one hour before the event start time; dress casually; have fun."

- When filling volunteer slots, succinctly state your request in the subject line of the e-mail similar to The Loft's most recent plea, "Still need two volunteers for Loft upcoming events. Please & thank you."

- Include a link to your event calendar where volunteers or those considering volunteering can go for more information about the event.

- Always, always include the contact person's name, e-mail address and phone number. Make it easy for volunteers to enlist.

- Repeat the mantra "short, sweet, inclusive, clear," while creating your e-newsletter.

Source: Dara Syrkin, Associate Communications Director/Volunteer Coordinator/Editor, A View from the Loft, The Loft Literary Center, Minneapolis, MN. E-mail: dsyrkin@loft.org.

This electronic newsletter keeps persons informed of upcoming opportunities to volunteer at The Loft Literary Center (Minneapolis, MN) with brief, specific information and directions on how to sign up or learn more.

Content not available in this edition

Engage Members With Interactive E-Newsletters

Spicing up your e-newsletter is a simple yet effective way to get members to engage, connect and renew. Instead of pushing content that doesn't stand out to subscribers, why not make e-newsletters fun and informative? That is what the Ronald Reagan Presidential Foundation did to communicate with its members. Associate Director of Membership Angie Bartel provides tips for going interactive:

Pick a Theme — Choosing a specific theme for each newsletter makes it easier to select interactive activities. For example, the foundation takes current events like the space shuttle program and debt ceiling and links them back to events in the Reagan presidency.

Include Fun and Freebies — Activities like trivia and crossword puzzles are a fun way to share information and get members to interact. Also, members are accustomed to always being asked for money, time or other commitments.

Use the newsletter to give back. "We provide free Reagan-themed computer wallpaper, Reagan conservative talking points, a weekly quote e-mail, and a recipe of the month for members only," she says. "All are free, furthering connections and adding member value."

Make it Exclusive — Give members the inside scoop and make them feel like they are part of something exclusive. However, make it easy for them to invite others to join by providing an Invite link.

One of the benefits of an interactive newsletter is increased click-throughs. The heightened attention it demands from members drives website traffic and increases the value your organization offers.

Source: Angie Bartel, Associate Director of Membership, Ronald Reagan Presidential Foundation, Simi Valley, CA.
E-mail: abartel@reaganfoundation.org

Communicate Fundraising Achievements With a Thermometer

Consider adding a fundraising thermometer illustrating your campaign's progress to your e-newsletter, website, blog or other electronic communications. This simple graphic lets donors and potential donors know where your campaign stands with a quick glance.

Fundraiser Insight (Guelph, Ontario, Canada) offers free, personalized fundraiser thermometers in vertical, horizontal and themed formats that can be added to websites, e-mails, social media and other communications pieces. As your funds

grow, the advancing donations can be reflected using Fundraiser Insight's visual thermometers.

Themed thermometers include visuals that are in the shape of a school bus, growing plant (shown at right), church steeple and others.

Find more information about free fundraising thermometers at www.fundraiserinsight.org/thermometer.

Source: Fundraiser Insight, Guelph, Ontario, Canada.

Content not available in this edition

Create Effective Podcasts

Creating video or audio podcasts on topics relevant to your mission is yet another way to connect with key audiences.

At Access to Student Assistance Programs in Reach of Everyone (ASPIRE; www.aspireoregon.org), Eugene, OR, officials create podcasts to communicate with constituents. ASPIRE is a mentoring program that offers volunteers the opportunity to mentor high school students regarding their college options.

To create effective podcasts, says Lori Ellis, ASPIRE and outreach supervisor:

1. Create a template that includes a consistent opening and closing that supports your agency's mission.

2. Maintain an engaging tone and avoid a dry delivery.

3. Use podcasts to provide information on specific topics that a variety of audiences would benefit from or that will help provide training for volunteers.

4. Use short time frames for presenting information. Ellis says she has found that anywhere from three to seven minutes allows them to present information easily absorbed by audiences.

5. Create a podcast studio in which to record your podcasts to limit interruptions.

6. Invest in microphones, webcams and software to make the most of the recording experience.

Source: Lori Ellis, ASPIRE and Outreach Supervisor, Access to Student Assistance Programs in Reach of Everyone, Eugene, OR.
E-mail: lorianne.m.ellis@state.or.us.

Executive Blog Plays Role In Communication Strategy

Should your president or CEO make time for a blog?

Raynard Kington, president of Grinnell College (www.grinnell.edu) in Grinnell, IA, does, and says it's a valuable facet of a comprehensive communication strategy. He answers questions about his blog (www.grinnell.edu/offices/president/blog):

How did the idea originate?

"When I arrived at Grinnell as an incoming president last fall, I scheduled a 'town meeting' at which I talked about some things that I thought were important for the college community to know and think about. Someone said they liked the town meeting very much, but wondered about the people who weren't able to attend. I said I would do everything I could to communicate with the community as often as possible. I said something like, 'I suppose I could even blog.' Someone in the communication office offered to help produce one, and we started working on it right away."

How much time does it take?

"Not much. A communication staff person takes notes during my addresses to campus or during a meeting with me and, based on those notes, writes drafts of monthly blog entries for my review. I edit the drafts, and the communication office publishes them to the website. The same staffer also monitors blog feedback and comments, which are unpublished, and forwards them to me for my review."

Are there any drawbacks to consider before starting a blog?

"Blogs require a commitment to regular, authentic, two-way communication and a comfort with the blog form. Blogs are, by their first-person nature, a somewhat informal, personal, intimate communication. They are not a series of press releases or institutional statements; they must convey the voice and persona of the blogger, or they won't be perceived as authentic. That doesn't mean the blogger has to write every word, but it does mean that the blogger must have a clear sense of his or her own voice and message and ensure that these are translated pitch-perfect to the blog."

Source: Daniel Weeks, Editorial Director, Office of College and Alumni Relations, Grinnell College, Grinnell, IA. E-mail: weeksdan@grinnell.edu.

Diversify the Aim, Appeal of Member Blogs

Of the many technologies that transformed organizational communication from a one-directional monologue to interactive and member-based dialogue, few are more important than blogs. Blogs helped break down traditional barriers and allow members to take an active role in communicating on issues of concern to them.

In the past, a single blog provided a sufficient space for interaction and input. Today, however, more nuance is required. To engage the widest segment of your membership, consider offering a variety of blogs targeting different member subcultures and constituent groups.

The American Library Association (Chicago, IL) provides a good example. The website of its official magazine, American Libraries (http://americanlibrariesmagazine.org/blogs), hosts a variety of blogs on eight different topic areas.

The Global Reach blog, for example, shares news and perspectives from libraries around the world. The Student Member blog reaches out to young people by addressing the concerns of aspiring professionals. The Ask the ALA Librarian blog encourages member interaction and collaboration with a question-and-answer format.

This diversity of content lets members follow the topics most interesting to them. An All Blogs feature facilitates further dialogue by compiling and displaying postings from all categories, regardless of subject matter.

If you are looking to enhance interaction with your members, consider adding additional blogs of interest to particular demographics or groups.

Websites Offer Designer Social Media Buttons

Icons used to promote social media initiatives can be simple or extravagant, elegant or outrageous. To find buttons that match your organization's personality, check out:

- **www.buttonshut.com** — provides multiple pages of buttons for well-known services like Facebook and LinkedIn plus but up-and-comers like Bebo, StumbleUpon and Reddit.

- **www.twitterbuttons.com** — offers dozens of Twitter button options.

- **www.webdesignerdepot.com/2010/10/ultimate-collection-of-social-media-icons** — includes a collections of buttons grouped into descriptive categories.

- **www.opensourcehunter.com/2008/10/11/social-buttons** — provides an index of third-party pages offering sets of social icons and buttons.

Avoid Headaches With Blogging Disclosure Policies

Blogs and other social media are essential for reaching out to members, donors, supporters and the public. But they also present new and evolving challenges. As organizational blogs become ever more informal and greater numbers of employees tweet, post and blog about the causes they support, the line between official and private communications becomes increasingly blurred.

Formulating clear disclosure policies to regulate employee conduct in social media venues can help prevent public misunderstandings and embarrassing missteps. Such policies should address a range of new media, including formal organizational communications (e.g., an official Facebook page), personal communications (e.g., an employee's personal blog) and interaction with external social media sources (e.g., commenting on an industry discussion board).

Wondering where to begin? The Disclosure Best Practices Toolkit developed by SocialMedia.org (Chicago, IL) provides one starting point. Excerpts of this resource — which can be found in its entirety at www.socialmedia.org/disclosure and can be freely used and adapted under the Creative Commons Attribution 3.0 License — are pictured below.

Source: SocialMedia.org, Chicago, IL.

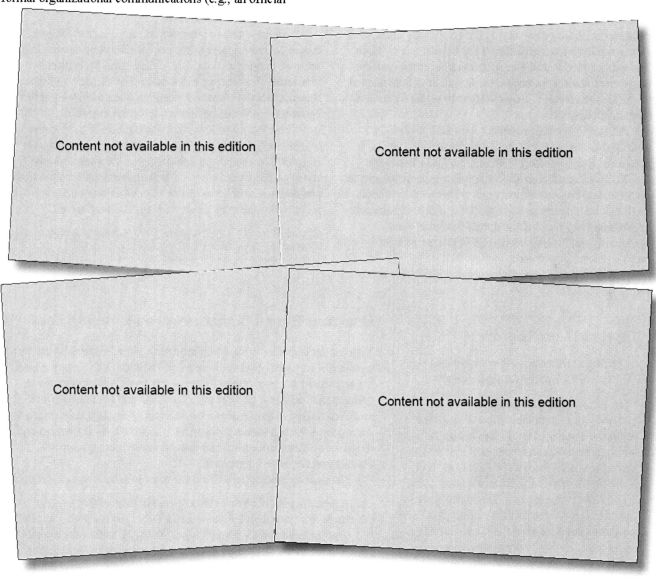

Content not available in this edition

Content not available in this edition

Content not available in this edition

Content not available in this edition

'Simple but Powerful' Video Proves Invaluable Fundraising Tool

A video presentation is credited with helping The Holland Hospital Foundation (Holland, MI) add 20 new businesses to its donor ranks and increase its donor base by 40 percent during a time of recession.

Foundation Executive Director Sue Ann Culp says, "Michigan has the second largest unemployment rate in the nation, and still, we have experienced increases, unlike other nonprofits in this area who are struggling to survive."

Culp credits that growth, in part, to a "simple but powerful" video presentation.

Created using Microsoft PowerPoint, the video includes the foundation's mission statement and an overview of its three focus areas of funding: 1) school nursing, 2) the community health center, and 3) the community nurse who serves at a local homeless shelter for women and children. The video includes statistics supporting community need, usage and outcome for each area, as well as dollars needed to sustain the services. It concludes with a plea for help and contact information.

All staff carry the presentation on flash drives, on their laptops and in DVD and DVR formats to share with prospects. Culp says they also send the DVD to donors.

Foundation officials show the video in presentations to corporations, businesses, grantors and prospective donors, as well as at community gatherings like chamber of commerce breakfasts. They highlight it at the foundation's major community fundraising events and in orientations for hospital employees and physicians.

The communications tool is proving invaluable for the foundation, Culp says, especially given its low production cost. "The only cost associated with producing this presentation was staff time, and a disc of stock photos. Its shelf life is infinite as long as our focus areas remain the same, since we can easily change statistics and numbers year to year."

"... make sure the message, music and imaging are strongly emotional, personal and cohesive, so it flows seamlessly."

For organizations seeking to invest time and effort in a similar video project, Culp recommends adding elements exclusive to your organization.

"We have named our mission The FACE of Holland Project, Funding Access to Care for Everyone, so the images we used in our video are lots of faces, and faces draw the viewer in. The background song is 'The Prayer' by Celtic Woman, which reflects the deep religious overtones of this community without being overtly denominational.

"The trick to producing a presentation of this type is to make sure the message, music and imaging are strongly emotional, personal and cohesive, so it flows seamlessly," she says. "The ask at the end is the natural culmination of the presentation, and the evidence of need is overwhelming. The pictures tell the story better than any narrator could."

Source: Sue Ann Culp, Executive Director, Holland Hospital Foundation, Holland, MI.
E-mail: saculp@hollandhospital.org

Try Hands-on Approach

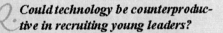

Could technology be counterproductive in recruiting young leaders?

"Yes, in some cases. Young leaders are inundated with e-mail invitations. This group needs to be engaged with a hands-on, exclusive opportunity, and the invitation needs to come personally from a peer. Your best tool is the first dozen young leaders spreading the word. How to engage that first dozen? Call the interested younger family members of your current donor base. Online invitations and e-mails can come back into the communication cycle once your members are committed to your cause and name recognition is achieved."

— Erin Meade, Development Officer,
The Methodist Hospital Group (Houston, TX)

Use Your E-mail Signature as a Marketing Tool

Your e-mail signature (a feature within most e-mail programs) can be a powerful way to market your organization. Attached to every e-mail, the signature has the potential to carry your name, title, organization name, e-mail address, mailing address, phone and fax numbers, website and even a short message to every e-mail recipient. If you belong to a discussion list, each message you send is archived, so that even months down the road someone may find your archived message and want to contact you for more information.

Here are some tips for making the most of your e-mail signature:

1. A signature should be no longer than six lines of text.
2. Include http:// before your web address so the recipient can reach your website simply by clicking on the URL within the e-mail.
3. Include your full contact information: name, title, organization name, mailing address, phone and fax numbers, e-mail address and website.
4. Include a short message. For example, a line advertising your upcoming event, a tip related to your service or a request for a donation and a link to your secure online donation site.

Rules for Sending E-mail Asks to Couples

Q. Should annual fund electronic appeals go to both spouses or just one?

"We e-mail both the primary donor and spouse if they both have active e-mail addresses, and we segment based on the highest priority constituent code. We also made a decision to be inclusive in personalization, since some families use a shared address, others use individual ones, and we don't have any way of knowing that. So we use an informal household salutation (Dear Joe and Jane) regardless of which person has the e-mail address on his/her record."

— Rendi Hahn, Advancement Campaign Coordinator and Prospect Manager, Abilene Christian University (Abilene, TX)

"If both constituents have a relationship with the organization (which they would if you have different e-mail addresses for each), then you should e-mail them separately. If you just happen to have the spouse name for invitations and honor roll listings, but the relationship is only with one person, then you should only e-mail your primary contact."

— Debra Holcomb, Director of Alumni Relations & Services, University of California, San Francisco (San Francisco, CA)

"We send only one e-mail if spouses share the same preferred e-mail address. If the preferred e-mail addresses do not match, then we send two messages and put a 'CC' at the bottom of each e-mail containing the spouse's e-mail address so that each knows that we wrote to the other person, too. We use a joint salutation in both cases (assuming that both spouses fall into the target audience for the particular appeal)."

— Tammie Ruda, Executive Director of Annual Giving, Brown University (Providence, RI)

Drive Video-based Fundraising With mailVU

"Video mail is much more effective than text e-mail in getting fundraising support," says Alan Fitzpatrick, CEO and co-founder of mailVU (Charlotte, NC) — which is why his for-profit business chooses to give away its services to nonprofits for free.

Nonprofits and individuals can use mailVU (www.mailVU.com) to send video messages up to 10 minutes in length in the body of an e-mail at no cost. (The business's for-profit clients pay for these and other, more customized services.) Users can either record straight from their webcams, or send more sophisticated videos that they've recorded and edited using other technology. There is no account to sign up for and nothing to upload or download.

"The mailVU founders are experts in Internet video and recognized the lack of an easy-to-use method of recording and distributing to any Web-enabled device," says Fitzpatrick. Towards that end, mailVU also offers a free iPhone app on iTunes, allowing users to create and send free video messages using only their smartphones or tablets.

On the receiving end, your video message's recipients will be able to watch your message no matter what type of computer or PDA they have. Explains Fitzpatrick, "mailVU determines the device type accessing the video and plays the appropriate code (coder-decoder) version." Fitzpatrick also stresses that no information technology knowledge is needed to implement a video campaign.

In 2010, the Charlotte Jewish Day School (CJDS; www.cjdschool.org) of Charlotte, NC, used mailVU's service to win $500,000 in a nationwide fundraising competition, in which the winners were determined based on an online voting contest. "A major benefit of CJDS using mailVU was to push video messages directly to the recipients' in-boxes," says Fitzpatrick. "Asking people to go to a website or YouTube is not as effective as pushing the content directly to the person ... Video messages are opened at a rate three times higher than text e-mails."

"Asking people to go to a website or YouTube is not as effective as pushing the content directly to the person ... Video messages are opened at a rate three times higher than text e-mails."

Gale Osborne, CJDS development director, says that mailVU's video messaging service was used during the last three weeks of the school's seven-week get-out-the-vote campaign as a successful final push. "Throughout the campaign we inundated people's mailboxes with typical e-mails," Osborne says. "I think that people opened these (mailVU) e-mails because they were unique."

Sources: Alan Fitzpatrick, Co-founder and CEO, mailVU, Charlotte, NC. E-mail: afitzpatrick@mailvu.com.
Gale Osborne, Development Director, Charlotte Jewish Day School, Charlotte, NC. E-mail: gosborne@cjdschool.org.

Online Fundraising Essentials, Second Edition.
Edited by Scott C. Stevenson.
© 2012 Stevenson, Inc. Published 2012 by Stevenson, Inc.

SHARE EVER-CHANGING FUNDING OPPORTUNITIES

Use your website and online communications to share a variety of ever-changing gift opportunities (and gift ranges) with your constituents. Such funding opportunities can be shared through wish lists, naming opportunities, examples of what others have done, campaign projects and more.

Engage Donors With Multiple Online Giving Options

To simplify online giving and keep potential donors engaged in the process, officials at Fort Lewis College (Durango, CO) recently revamped its online giving form.

The form (https://apps.fortlewis.edu/makeagift/Gift.aspx) now features a drop-down menu format with 251 options in eight categories donors use to direct gifts.

By helping people quickly find desired funding areas, the selection tool removes one barrier that keeps donors from giving, says David Smith, annual fund manager.

"We want to make the online gift process as easy as possible," Smith says. He notes that they were motivated to simplify the process after potential donors informed them they were not donating online because they were not seeing the particular fund(s) to which they wished to donate.

As a result, Smith says they chose to include all funds, separated into categories, with a search engine and an Other choice for persons seeking to fund an area not listed. They also created a giving page for potential donors to view prior to making a gift, which provides links and details on the various options for giving.

To further simplify donating online, foundation staff worked with the college's information technology department to create hyperlinks to the online giving form, says Smith, which they now typically place in e-communications as well.

Since going live with the online revamp, Smith says visits to the online giving form have stayed relatively steady, at about 160 per month. "Feedback has been overwhelmingly positive. Donors are happy to have the monthly installment option available and college entities are happy to have their funds listed within the form."

To continue promoting online giving and simplifying the process, Smith says, they plan to create promotional postcards and a donor-based e-newsletter with additional hyperlinks, as well as have on-campus entities that are listed within the online giving form create links from their websites to the form.

Source: David Smith, Annual Fund Manager, Fort Lewis College, Durango, CO. E-mail: SMITH_DAVID@fortlewis.edu

Quick Gifts Page Supports Mission, Offers Marketing Venue

Creating a Quick Gifts page on your nonprofit's website is a great option to promote ways for constituents to support your cause while offering your organization a unique marketing opportunity.

UniversalGiving (San Francisco, CA) offers its supporters a Quick Gift page at http://www.universalgiving.org/quickGift. do that outlines ways in which they can support the nonprofit's mission. On this page, constituents can select from a broad range of donation amounts in the name of a friend or loved one.

Pamela Hawley, founder and CEO of UniversalGiving, shares the concept behind the Quick Gift Web page:

What is the overall purpose of your Quick Gifts page?

"We offer many gift options allowing supporters to give to a person in need on behalf of a loved one. Searching our gift package database, supporters can browse by cause, region or choose from our top gift packages. These gifts cover a wide range of social issues, from the environment, to poverty, to human rights, making it easy to choose a cause a loved one cares about. Supporters can send a soccer ball to an impoverished child for just $15, empower a woman entrepreneur in South America for $100, or sponsor a student in Tanzania for $500. Gift certificates are also available. For those in a rush, the Quick Gifts page allows someone to purchase 20 gifts with one click, choosing several gifts for multiple friends all at once. A purchaser can also personalize the gift and the message to each friend."

How do you determine the pricing of your Quick Gifts items and what draws people to this page?

"We feature a range of options, so anyone can find an amount to fit their budget. We also let the nonprofits we support drive pricing according to their needs. Many people have tighter budgets during this difficult economic time. And yet, people still want to give gifts to each other. What we're also seeing is that people want their giving to be more meaningful. So rather than spending $100 for a shirt or purse, they can give $25 to offer someone clean water or $30 to feed a child for a month."

What tips could you share with other nonprofits who wish to initiate a Quick Gifts page?

"It's quick, it's innovative and it's great creative marketing! Nonprofits need to offer quality trusted ways for people to give, and they need to market this opportunity smartly. Quick Gifts allows a nonprofit to promote and receive more donations, because people feel it serves many purposes. They can give a meaningful gift, support a cause, get a tax write-off, and know that their gift is making an impact; these are also benefits a nonprofit can note to promote its Quick Gifts Web page. As a nonprofit starting a Quick Gifts page, we recommend focusing on quick, concise, peppy writing that will attract your donor and make them want to support the cause."

Source: Pamela Hawley, Founder and CEO, and Cheryl Mahoney, Marketing Associate, UniversalGiving, San Francisco, CA. E-mail: phawley@universalgiving.org.

Increase Donors' Ability to Give With an In-kind Wish List

While nonprofits prefer gifts of unrestricted cash, but sometimes in-kind donations are all that supporters can manage. Similarly, some individuals are motivated by seeing exactly what their contribution provides.

Officials at the Signature Theatre (Arlington, VA) first sought to realize the potential of large-scale in-kind donations in the spring of 2010. Though they had received catered food and décor in the past, they wanted to bolster direct theatre operations, says Erin Harms, associate director of development.

"Supplies for sets, structures, construction tools, video equipment — we took almost anything we could get," says Harms. "Any in-kind contribution offsets a budgeted expense, so there's no reason not to seek them."

An online wish list (pictured in part, right) is the centerpiece of the theatre's in-kind outreach efforts. The well-designed list increases the likelihood of donation by effectively employing a few basic strategies. These include:

- **Segmented costs.** The theatre's wish list is broken down by price into four levels of donation, giving a range of options for every budget.

- **Evocative descriptions.** Unlike lists that offer little or no description of items, the theatre's list clearly explains why an item is needed and how it furthers the organization's mission. Friendly and humorous writing draws attention and helps build emotional connections with potential supporters.

- **Clickable links to direct purchase.** Every item on the theatre's list is linked to a retail website such as

www.target.com or www.dell.com. This provides exact specifications on all items and allows supporters to order them on the spot, if they wish.

Source: Erin Harms, Associate Director of Development, Signature Theatre, Arlington, VA. E-mail: harmse@signature-theatre.org.

SIGNATURE'S WISH LIST

Please click on the item name below to be linked to a detailed description of the item

Gifts for Under $100

STAPLE "GUN" for the Scene Shop
Sets have to be put up and taken down quickly, but remain sturdy throughout a 6 to 8 week run of performances — what's the secret? Staples! Drop off your new or slightly used staple guns (1" Narrow or Medium Crown). Heavy-duty staples are also welcome!

COPY PAPER for Scripts
Sure, everyone uses it — but no one department uses it more than the Production and Artistic Team! Each actor, designer, assistant, and technician needs a copy of every script we do — and some, like the Stage Management team, need more than one copy. Help keep us ahead of the demand by donating reams and cases of paper — it's a little thing that makes a big difference.

Gifts from $100 to $500

17" FLAT SCREEN MONITOR (Quantity 3)
Help our employees stop squinting at outdated screens and make more room on their desks with these space saving computer monitors. If you've recently upgraded your monitor, drop your old monitor off and you'll receive a donation receipt that can help you save money on taxes. Multiple items will be readily accepted!

Gifts from $500 to $1,000

FLOOR DRILL PRESS for the Scene Shop
Drop off a new or slightly used floor drill press in good condition and you'll have our carpenters saying "Drill Baby Drill!"

DELL OPTIPLEX COMPUTERS
In business these days, it seems like you can never have too many computers — and theatre is no exception! Drop off your new or used machines that meet the minimum requirements: Windows XP Professional Operating System, 2.1 GHZ or greater processor, 1GB or more RAM (2 GB preferred) and get a donation receipt that can help you on your taxes.

Gifts from $1,000 +

VectorWorks Licenses for PC (Quantity 2)
Ever wonder what software designers use to draw up scenic and lighting designs? Signature uses VectorWorks, one of two of the most popular AutoCAD drafting programs. Licenses for this amazing software are expensive. Help offset the cost by donating one today.

Registries Take Guess Work Out of Wish Lists

Looking to delegate the coordination of your organization's wish list? Set it up through a store registry.

Just like blushing brides and moms-to-be, your organization can set up a list of the things you want (and need)!

Then, all you have to do is let your followers know about it through your website, social networks and publications. The store keeps track of what has already been bought, you can add things at any time and all of the items will be new.

Donor-centric Catalog Lets Prospects Browse Giving Choices

Are you looking for a one-stop resource for donors and development staff alike? Consider the giving catalog produced by the University of Pittsburgh (Pittsburgh, PA).

Jasmine Hoffman, manager of public relations in institutional advancement, says that since its inception in December 2008, the online catalog has received more than 1,200 unique page views and is the seventh most-visited page on the site.

Hoffman says the most interesting analysis though is in the page's bounce rate.

"The bounce rate measures the number of people who leave the site after viewing only one page," she says. "Eighty-seven percent of the users who visit the giving catalog are navigating through multiple pages in the catalog. The giving catalog is providing prospective donors with quality information about giving, while they research their philanthropic interests."

So how does the giving catalog work?

Prospective donors visit the website at www.giveto.pitt. edu/catalog/index.asp through an easy link on the home page of the university's website. There they are able to research giving opportunities through four filters: university priorities, dollar amount, key words and build your own gift. Once they have reviewed their options, they can be linked directly to a development officer. "Inquiries go directly to the development officer who is fundraising for that particular initiative.

"The site also allows development staff to quickly send information to prospective donors. For instance, if a donor wants more information about a Student Resources Fund in the School of Arts and Sciences, the development officer can quickly e-mail an information sheet about that gift to a donor," says Hoffman.

Hoffman says their primary goal in developing the catalog was to serve as an information source for donors and development officers. "It's doing that and more. Feedback so far has been positive, with users finding the catalog intuitive and easy to use."

Source: Jasmine Hoffman, Manager of Public Relations in Institutional Advancement, University of Pittsburgh, Pittsburgh, PA.
E-mail: jasmine.hoffman@ia.pitt.edu

Naming Opportunities Boost Campaign Appeal

"We have found that naming opportunities are one of the most powerful ways of securing major gifts," says H. Ken DeDominicis, vice president for institutional advancement, University of St. Thomas (Houston, TX).

To that end, the university's primary strategy is to use naming opportunities to subsidize the building. DeDominicis says, "If you tally up all of the naming opportunities suggested online, you will find that the sum is much larger than $75M. We received half a million dollars from a local foundation solely for developing the drawings and plans for constructing the new facility. In working with the architects, we developed an extensive segmentation of naming opportunities along with illustrations provided mainly by the architectural firm. We then determined the reasonable sum for each of the naming opportunities based on our collective experience and the local market."

The naming opportunities are being marketed online, as well as through personal presentations to potential donors. The university's donor community and alumni are also being alerted to these opportunities through electronic media. Officials are hoping to secure the lead gift, which would be to name the center, over the next eighteen months. DeDominicis says securing that gift will enable them to leverage other major gifts required for a successful campaign.

Source: H. Ken DeDominicis, Vice President for Institutional Advancement, University of St. Thomas, Houston, TX.
E-mail: ken@stthom.edu

Pictured here is the list shown on the University of St. Thomas website describing available naming opportunities.

Content not available in this edition

Online Fundraising Essentials, Second Edition.
Edited by Scott C. Stevenson.
© 2012 Stevenson, Inc. Published 2012 by Stevenson, Inc.

Online Fundraising Essentials — 2ⁿᵈ Edition

INVITE DIVERSE TYPES OF GIVING

In addition to sharing a variety of gift opportunities, cover all bases with regard to types of giving: restricted gifts, planned gifts, sponsorships, annual support, matching gifts and more. Think of your website as a menu offering several entrees that appeal to a wide variety of interests and financial abilities.

Virtual Food Drive Collects $9,000

For a fun, low-cost way to raise money, consider a virtual food drive similar to the one launched by the Food Bank of South Jersey (Pennsauken, NJ).

"Let's Do Lunch is a community-wide initiative that asks participating companies' employees to donate what they would normally spend on lunch one or more days that week to the Food Bank of South Jersey to help feed South Jersey's hungry," says Mario Partee, corporate partnerships manager. "Participants make selections from the menu. The total cost for the items they have chosen will be the amount the participant will be asked to donate. This allows participants to see the impact of their giving."

Partee explains how the program works:

- Food bank staff recruit local companies to participate in the program. The companies then encourage employees to participate.

- Food bank staff set up the virtual drive link for employees to access online. A printed menu with food items is available for persons who do not have Internet access.

- Persons log on or fill out paperwork, selecting what they would like for "lunch." Choices determine dollar amount they would like to contribute. Donors can pay online by credit card or offline by check,

cash or money order to a designated staff person.

- At week's end, the food bank staff tallies donations per participant. Some companies have a friendly competition to see which department raises the most funds.

The program's Thanksgiving/Holiday 2008 drive raised $9,000 from 122 participants. Partee says the fundraiser requires little investment other than set-up time, and adds that many people respond better to this method than traditional direct mail appeals.

Source: Mario Partee, Corporate Partnerships Manager, Food Bank of South Jersey, Pennsauken, NJ. E-mail: mpartee@foodbanksj.org

An interactive website pledge form helps people give to the online food drive for the Food Bank of South Jersey (Pennsauken, NJ).

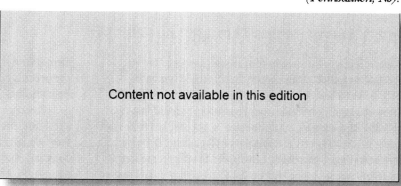

Content not available in this edition

Blackbaud Tool Helps Take Fundraising Online

When staff at My Sister's House, Inc. (Charleston, SC) decided to launch a campaign urging supporters to donate five dollars within five days, they evaluated several options, including deploying changes to the organization's national website.

Instead, they chose BlackbaudNow as a fast and easy option to get online and start accepting donations.

In just five days, the organization raised more than $6,000, mostly online.

BlackbaudNow is extremely user-friendly, says Elmire Raven, executive director of My Sister's House, Inc. "You go to the site, set up your user name and password and develop your information. In an hour, the website was designed and went live. It was very simple."

So what is BlackbaudNow? It's a point-and-click website builder for nonprofits and personal fundraisers. It provides

secure donation processing through PayPal, along with the ability to send e-mails and record donors' giving histories. Users pay fees on a per-transaction basis.

Nonprofit representatives can visit www.blackbaudnow.com to register for a free web seminar introducing BlackbaudNow or see frequently asked questions, including pricing and additional details, at www.bbnow.com/resources/faqs/.

While recommending exploring the website to be sure it meets all of your needs and expectations for the task you would like it to perform, Raven notes that in the case of My Sister's House, Inc., they were able to easily work through any glitches they faced with BlackbaudNow. "We have used it three times. It is awesome!"

Source: Elmire Raven, Executive Director, My Sister's House, Inc., North Charleston, SC. E-mail: eraven@mysistershouse.com

Online Search Tool Promotes Matching Gift Opportunities

Sometimes, the potential to double a donor gift is just a mouse click away.

Visitors to the website for KUHF Houston Public Radio (Houston, TX) can use an online search tool to quickly learn if their company has a matching gift program.

Using the Employer Matching Gift search tool offered by HEP Development (Leesburg, VA), visitors to www.kuhf.org enter their company name into the search bar. Search results include:

- ❑ Company   ❑ Subsidiary of   ❑ Foundation #
- ❑ Gift ratio   ❑ Comments section
- ❑ Matching gifts procedure
- ❑ Matching Gift Form URL.
- ❑ When information was last updated.
- ❑ Matching gift program contact person.
- ❑ Phone and e-mail address for the matching gift program.
- ❑ Minimum/maximum amount matched.
- ❑ Total amount matched per employee.

HEP staff maintain and regularly update the list of matching gift companies.

Suzanne Tullis, KUHF director of individual giving, says they have used the search tool for two years. "We used to have to keep the list of companies that provide matching gifts up-to-date ourselves and then regularly mail it to our constituents," she says. "This is a more convenient, simple and cost-saving solution."

Stephen P. Hafner, HEP Development founder and CEO, says the search tool is just one important part of an overall best-practices matching gift strategy. Other services include appending employer data for nonprofits and then determining if the firm is match eligible which allows the nonprofit to grow its pool of match revenue.

"We can also mine a nonprofit's existing employer data to see if the company matches, so that they can target the donor for a match," he says. The search tool is also a stand-alone product, says Hafner, selling for $600 to $1,000 per year.

Sources: Stephen P. Hafner, Founder & CEO, HEP Development, Leesburg, VA. E-mail: steve@hepdata.com.
Suzanne Tullis, Director of Individual Giving, KUHF Houston Public Radio, Houston, TX. E-mail: stullis@kuhf.org

Invite Sponsorships Through Your Website

Recruiting area businesses to sponsor an event may be as easy as a click of the mouse. In March, Morrisville, NC, added a new sponsorship page to the town's website (www.townofmorrisville.org/sponsorship). In the first two months of operation, 10 businesses sponsored events in the town of 18,000 people, raising about $10,000. "It seems to be working," says Matt Leaver, the town's recreation superintendent, noting that before the Web page only one or two businesses would sponsor events in some years.

In addition to providing information on what events a business can sponsor, the site describes the recognition companies will receive for their sponsorship dollars. Within each category, a business can select its level of sponsorship, ranging from $50 to $3,000. "Each event has a different range of sponsorship levels. It depends what the budget is for each event as to how much sponsorship money is needed," says Leaver.

Stephanie Smith, public information officer for Morrisville is in charge of securing these sponsorships with area businesses. She says many businesses want to sponsor events but don't know how to go about it. "When we first launched the website, we sent a mass postcard mailing to all area businesses with a privilege license from the town to let

them know about the website. This way they could visit the site at their convenience and fill out an online interest form," says Smith.

The online interest form lists all the sponsorship opportunities, so a company can check the box of the event they are interested in sponsoring. The form also asks for the company name, contact person and contact information. It doesn't, however, ask for any dollar amounts. Smith says when a business fills out the interest form online, she contacts the company directly to discuss that information.

Both Leaver and Smith agree that having a sponsorship website has helped the town become more efficient and streamlined in its relationship with sponsors. "This way, all sponsors are treated equally. And to help with this consistency, it helps to have one person as a point of contact who follows up with sponsorship inquiries from the website," says Leaver.

Sources: Matt Leaver, Recreation Superintendent, Town of Morrisville, Morrisville, NC.
E-mail: mleaver@townofmorrisville.org.
Stephanie Smith, Public Information Officer, Town of Morrisville, Morrisville, NC. E-mail: ssmith@townofmorrisville.org

Detailed Planning Tools Make for Planned Giving Success

Well-thought-out strategies, accompanied by well-crafted written plans, can make all the difference when it comes to raising major gifts.

Officials at the American Association of Equine Practitioners (AAEP) Foundation, Lexington, KY, recently launched a planned giving program. That comes after a year of laying the internal groundwork necessary to make sure there was organizational readiness and commitment to such a program, says Development Coordinator Jodie Bingham. That year of laying the crucial groundwork included "making a concentrated effort to let people know we are deserving and ready to accept those kinds of gifts," she adds.

Two tools crucial to development of the program are the foundation's Planned Giving Timeline and Checklist of Essential Actions (below), and Infrastructure Checklist (right).

The timeline/checklist is a one-year plan that led up to the kickoff luncheon of the organization's new Legacy Society that recognizes persons who include the AAEP in estate plans. The checklist details what must be in place to support the society and accept planned gifts.

At the luncheon, foundation officials announced the society's seven charter members, featured the different planned giving options and highlighted the veterinarian who facilitated the original estate gift.

Following this concerted effort, Bingham says foundation officials are now prepared to facilitate planned giving by stating key information, highlighting people who are already committed, educating people on how easy planned giving can be and allaying prospects' concerns.

To further educate persons on planned giving, the foundation launched an interactive website (http://www.legacy.vg/aaep/giving/1.html) where they can assess their financial and prospective philanthropic status.

Since the launch of the Legacy Society, Bingham says, they have identified more than $1 million in planned gifts.

Source: Jodie Bingham, Development Coordinator, AAEP Foundation, Lexington, KY. Phone (859) 233-0147. E-mail: jbingham@aaep.org

Content not available in this edition

Content not available in this edition

Added Language Provides Gifting Details

Adding some simple language to your e-mail's automated out-of-office reply ensures that your organization can provide details on memorial gifts even when you are out.

Bonny Kellermann, director of memorial gifts, MIT (Cambridge, MA), includes the following in her auto-reply specifically to assist persons needing it for obituaries:

> "If you are looking for information to include in an obituary regarding memorial gifts, you can refer to the following language: 'In lieu of flowers, gifts may be made to MIT for the (name of fund). Checks should be payable to MIT and mailed to Bonny Kellermann, Director of Memorial Gifts; 600 Memorial Drive, W98-500; Cambridge, MA 02139. Please include a note stating that your gift is in memory of (name).' You can also reference the following webpage for additional information about memorial gifts: http://giving.mit.edu/ways/memoriam/."

Use similar language on your phone message and website to provide important information in a timely manner to families considering including memorial gift options in honor of a loved one who has passed away.

Source: Bonny Kellermann, Director of Memorial Gifts, MIT, Cambridge, MA. E-mail: bonnyk@MIT.EDU

Online Component Offers Boost to Brick Sales

By any standard, you could say the commemorative brick program (www.stlzoo.org/supportthezoo/tributescommemorativebrick.htm) at the Saint Louis Zoo (St. Louis, MO) has been a success. With more than 2,000 bricks sold to date, the program has netted $23,750 for the zoo in 2010.

Vice President of External Relations Cynthia Holter says offering a way for people to purchase bricks online has been critical to that success.

"Recently, since the zoo was not in a public campaign, approximately one third of brick donations came from the Internet. Having the information on the Internet allows people to have the information at their fingertips and order a brick 24/7. In this wired society we feel it is important to have this information readily available."

The bricks, used for pavers on one entrance to the plaza, are offered in a variety of sizes and styles wide enough to meet just about anyone's budget: 4" x 8" clay for $500; 4" x 8" bronze for $1,250; and 8" x 8" clay for $2,500, and an 8" x 8" bronze for $5,000.

Holter says it's most important to offer good quality bricks and an attractive pattern design for laying the bricks, so visitors will want to see their name or that of a loved one on a brick.

Source: Cynthia Holter, CFRE, Vice President of External Relations, Saint Louis Zoo, St. Louis, MO. E-mail: powell@stlzoo.org

Website Gives Faces to Callers, Reinforces Phonathon Efforts

As phone-based fundraising for Saint Vincent College (Latrobe, PA) grew, Director of Annual Fund Alicia Barnes sought to create a space to acknowledge student callers and educate people about the phonathon and the people who work to make it a success. The result is the website, Who's Calling You Tonight? (http://www.stvincent.edu/phonathon/meet-the-phonathon-callers).

"We started out small, with caller profiles, job information and phonathon scholarship information," Barnes says of the website. "It has grown to feature an online job application, recognition of companies who donate prizes, recognition of a caller of the week and senior phonathon students plus memories of past callers."

Barnes employs a graphic design student to maintain the website, updating caller profiles and phonathon sponsors. Bios are updated as callers come on board or graduate/leave the position. Callers select their profile picture and answer a set of questions, then send them off to be uploaded.

Callers are encouraged to promote the site while on the phone, says Barnes, "to advertise the site as well as put a face to a name."

Development staff also include the webpage link in pre-call solicitation letters.

Barnes says the website reflects positively on what student callers are trying to accomplish. "Overall, it is a positive reinforcement of what the phonathon does and what it stands for — the advancement of the college and future generations of Bearcats."

Source: Alicia M. Barnes, Director of Annual Fund, Saint Vincent College, Latrobe, PA. E-mail: alicia.barnes@email.stvincent.edu

Based on actual student caller profiles, this compilation shows information St. Vincent College shares on a website dedicated to its phonathon efforts:

Who's Calling You Tonight?

Name: Jane Doe

Hometown: Philadelphia, PA

Major: Mathematics

Activities/Hobbies: Reading, listening to music, studying.

Why you like being a Phonathon caller: Hearing about the experiences of alumni, working with other students and the friendly staff.

The best thing about SVC: People are so friendly here!

The sky's the limit (What you would love to do after college): Continue as a graduate student at SVC.

Six Key Strategies for Meeting a Once-in-a-lifetime Challenge

What would you do with an all-or-nothing, once-in-a-lifetime opportunity?

Development staff at Trinity College (Hartford, CT) recently faced that question with a challenge to beat all challenges: An anonymous donor promised an immediate $5 million gift, if they could achieve a gift participation rate of 55 percent or higher among Trinity's 20,000 living alumni. Failure to do so would mean the college would receive nothing.

In the end, the college achieved a giving rate of 55.34 percent, the highest alumni engagement rate among Connecticut institutions of higher education, and projected to be among the top 10 highest rates among two- and four-year colleges and universities across the country, says Gretchen Orschiedt, director of development.

Helping them accomplish this in just six short months, Orschiedt says, was the fact it was an all-or-nothing opportunity.

"All who volunteered and donated knew that it would be down to the last days that the challenge requirement would be met and that their help was critical," she says. "At Trinity, we do not receive $5 million gifts every day — this was a transformative endowment gift for the college — and all who were involved received this message."

To make sure all potential donors learned of this opportunity, Trinity staff:

1. **Employed extensive use of social media.** Trinity officials sent frequent Facebook messages and Twitter posts, including offering a Facebook Donor Badge to persons who gave online. They also e-mailed persons who made gifts before the challenge was announced, including an e-mail text that they could forward to all of their Trinity friends.

2. **Segmented donors.** This allowed specific individuals (e.g., faculty, coaches) to communicate the challenge message to a specific audience, such as former students or players.

3. **Brought goals to the class level.** Rather than focusing on the larger number needed to reach 55 percent participation, annual fund staff used individual class figures (e.g., "Your class is only 10 gifts away from reaching its goal!") to add emphasis to the need.

4. **Made sure recorded messages stood out.** A high-profile, famous alum and the associate director of athletics provided the unique voices for these calls that went out to remind prospective donors of the urgency of the message toward the end of the campaign.

5. **Provided weekly updates to volunteers on progress and need.** As the end of the campaign drew near these updates occured daily.

6. **Utilized additional resources.** Even volunteers not normally charged with soliciting, such as trustees, took on that role in this campaign. Volunteers received online resources (e.g., challenge case statement, Q&A and volunteer to-do list with easy steps to reach out to alumni about the challenge).

Source: Gretchen Orschiedt, Director of Development, Trinity College, Hartford, CT. E-mail: gretchen.orschiedt@trincoll.edu

---

Video Delivers Thanks for $5M Challenge Success

To thank all donors — especially those who helped reach an unprecedented $5 million alumni challenge gift from an anonymous donor — the annual fund team at Trinity College (Hartford, CT) turned to the college's communications team.

The result is a video showing those persons most impacted by donors' generosity — students with a wide range of academic and social interests — in locations throughout campus as they say, "Thank you!"

Director of Annual Giving Jocelyn Kane says the video includes a personal thank you from the college president and a whimsical story line featuring the college's mascot, the Trinity Bantam, presenting the president with a briefcase holding the $5 million.

The communications team created the video in-house using available equipment. The only external cost was $25 in music copyrights through a third-party website.

All alumni donors received an e-mail with a link to the video on YouTube (http://www.youtube.com/watch?v=331ndHIcAU0). If no e-mail address was available, donors were sent postcards with the video's website address. The link is also posted on the college website, www.trincoll.edu.

Source: Jocelyn Kane, Director of Annual Giving, Trinity College, Hartford, CT. E-mail: jocelyn.kane@trincoll.edu

Online Fundraising Essentials, Second Edition.
Edited by Scott C. Stevenson.
© 2012 Stevenson, Inc. Published 2012 by Stevenson, Inc.

The e-mail generation is hitting its prime and the Twitter/texting generation is not far behind, meaning tomorrow's donors will be more at home online than any before. Meet their needs with online events that not only raise funds but serve to build your online community and engage those who visit your website.

Twitter-driven Fundraiser Brings in $10,000 in 10 Days

Nonprofit organizations across the country have had varying degrees of success in harnessing the power of Twitter networking to bring in much-needed donations. Through these groups' trial and error, a best practices approach is emerging that can help you decide whether a Twitter-based fundraiser will work for you.

One successful group has been the ChristmasFuture Foundation (Calgary, Alberta, Canada), a Canadian-based nonprofit that funds projects worldwide to help erase extreme poverty. ChristmasFuture raised more than $10,000 in the 10 days before Christmas 2008 with its TweetmasFuture fundraiser, says operations manager Leif Baradoy. In all, it brought in about 7 percent of the group's annual budget.

"We've only really been around for two years as an organization, but the key to our success was that we have been able to powerfully represent ourselves through our projects," which include everything from youth arts and leadership programs in Nicaragua to funding a water sanitation project in Sierra Leone, Baradoy says.

The TweetmasFuture campaign didn't have a lot of planning involved, Baradoy says, but it did require a way to donate money online. They sent direct messages on Twitter to many of their 400-plus followers, asking them to donate and/or send out "tweets" (brief messages sent to subscribers through Twitter) about the campaign. All they had to do then was keep the word going.

Here are Baradoy's tips for a successful Twitter fundraiser:

✓ Invest in your followers: Those who have successfully raised thousands of dollars from Twitter activity all have something in common, Baradoy says — they have established a following on the social networking site for at least a year, and regularly send out useful updates (like articles, blog posts, etc., that relate to the organization's core mission) to engage their supporters in conversation. In other words, if you build trust with your social network, you build potential for a larger donation pool. "People will only share links and donate themselves, if they are convinced it is a good cause," he says.

✓ Keep it short: Any longer than 10 days is too long, Baradoy says. You don't want your campaign to become noise in the background.

✓ Give persons clear direction. In your initial message, state exactly what you would like them to do, which is to basically donate and retweet, Baradoy says. Don't try to say too much, as tweets are limited to 140 characters.

✓ Create a fundraiser Web page: The fundraiser should have its own Web page, and the link to that page should be included in every message you send for the event, Baradoy says. You can shorten the link through the use of computer applications like Tweetdeck, which will also help you keep track of your followers. Include your Twitter feed on that Web page, as well as publicity and links to other important aspects of your group. Make it easy for people to navigate and, of course, to donate.

✓ Use a hash tag to track the campaign: Hash tags allow Twitter users to search for all specific content related to that tag, so including one in each message related to the fundraiser is important if you want to see who's supporting you. Baradoy used #TweetmasFuture as a hash tag, but planned to shorten it for the 2009 effort.

✓ Follow up: Keep the word going by tweeting about how much money has been raised. Chances are those will be passed on, as well. Publicly thank those who have donated and/or retweeted your messages by sending a reply on Twitter. Consistent involvement in a Twitter campaign is fundamental to success, Baradoy says.

✓ Don't just take, give back: ChristmasFuture bought some of its own online donation gift certificates and sent them to the most involved Twitter followers. They could make a donation in their name or pass the gift along to a friend.

Contact: Leif Baradoy, Operations Manager, ChristmasFuture Foundation, Calgary, Alberta, Canada.
E-mail: info@christmasfuture.org

Tweeting For a Cause

Here is one sample of a tweet sent through www.twitter.com from a supporter of the ChristmasFuture Foundation (Calgary, Alberta, Canada) during a social network-driven fundraising effort in December 2008:

RT @sleenie: It's not too late to give... TweetmasFuture is still short of their goal. Check it out. http://tinyurl.com/66nzxq 12:18 PM Dec 23rd, 2008 from TweetDeck

---

Boost Results by Combining Live, Silent, Electronic Auctions

How does the GAMBIT Auction and Dinner of Canisius High School (Buffalo, NY) raise around $300,000 every year? Its 36-year history helps, but so does offering a variety of auction events, says Colleen Sellick, GAMBIT program coordinator.

The fundraiser begins months before the night of the event as parents and alumni hold up to a dozen parties to gather the 500 to 600 items auctioned every year. This extended season raises awareness of the auction and allows a wide range of supporters to become involved, says Sellick.

At the event, most gifts are distributed via silent auction. Items with bid sheets attached are displayed in five large groups that are progressively closed as the night proceeds. Larger items are reserved for the final group, and a grand finale offers a last chance at anything still available.

Following the silent auction, a live auction showcases two dozen of the most valuable and unusual gifts. Real-time action helps drive bids higher, says Sellick, and limiting the number of items offered helps retain interest and attention.

A gift website complements the traditional auction catalog as it displays all auction items and sorts them into categories to make navigation easier while allowing development staff to analyze the yield from different kinds of gifts and advise prospective donors accordingly. (Sellick says electronics, sports memorabilia, unique items and vacation homes generally offer great returns for their price.)

The school also began auctioning items directly online this year using the online Web service Maestrosoft (www.maestrosoft.com). So far Sellick has simply sold the items outright, but notes that another option involves using the highest online bid as the starting bid for on-site live or silent auctions.

While the online component is in trial stages, Sellick has already seen benefits.

"We have received donations and bids from around the country," she says. "In the future, this will be a great way to reach beyond our immediate community. And for now, just getting the word out about this feature has driven people to the website and increased our direct online donations, which is a great start!"

Source: Colleen Sellick, GAMBIT Coordinator, Canisius High School, Buffalo, NY. E-mail: Sellick@canisiushigh.org

Want to Make the Most of Your Silent Auction? Take It Online

Jon Carson, CEO of Bidding for Good (www.biddingforgood.com; Cambridge, MA), knows how to make silent auctions work with optimum efficacy.

Carson's business hosts online auctions for nonprofits using techniques gleaned from extensive research. "In person," Carson says, "silent auctions just don't work like they should." However, when that auction is moved online: "The same pair of sports tickets that sold in a silent auction for $450 will sell for $600. It's a matter of supply and demand."

Here, Carson explains how the Bidding for Good model works:

✓ **Timing.** According to Carson's associate Deepak Malhotra, assistant professor at Harvard Business School, live auctions are more successful than silent auctions because of competitive arousal. During a live auction, as stakes escalate, so does the competitive excitement, making participants more likely to bid, and bid higher. Silent auctions do almost the opposite: Research shows people dislike betting against friends while socializing, and there is no climactic finish at the close of the silent auction. "When you're at home viewing an online auction, that competitive arousal comes back," Carson says. "We know that in the last hour and a half of an online auction, bids spike considerably. It allows people to focus and get excited in a way they can't when they're writing on a clipboard in the middle of a crowded room."

✓ **Higher participation.** Auctions that are part of a gala event are only accessible to attendees of that event, who may represent only a fraction of the potential donor pool. Online auctions can reach anyone in the organization's community — and beyond — at any hour of the day or night.

✓ **Searchable items.** When people are able to find items they want and bypass items they don't, they are more likely to bid.

✓ **Better donations.** Due to the above factors, online auctions reach a broad base of people who are ready and willing to spend. Therefore, online auctions become attractive platforms for companies to donate auction items simply for the advertising opportunity. Free product equals pure profit for your organization.

✓ **Targeted techniques.** An online auction is a controlled environment, which means auctions can be tailored to match bidders' behavior. For instance, studies show that people are more likely to respond to bid alerts that appeal to their sense of charity, rather than their competition — until the auction is almost over. Another example: Research showed that women bid on more items than men do, while men bid higher and more competitively than women do. Online auctions can take factors like these into account and build them into their auction set-up.

Source: Jon Carson, CEO, Bidding for Good, Cambridge, MA. E-mail: jon@biddingforgood.com

Online Sports Auction Beats Event Planning for University

When it comes to raising funds, online auctions are hard to beat, says Whitey Rigsby, director, The V Club, Villanova University (Villanova, PA).

Through online auctions, "We've raised between $80,000 and $100,000 every year for the last five years, without the overhead or work involved with a large-scale event," Rigsby says. In fact, he says, for the first five years of the auction, responsibilities were so manageable that he and his secretary easily handled all of the necessary work.

The auction features sports memorabilia, vacation packages and once-in-a-lifetime opportunities, including the chance to travel with the men's basketball team to Louisville or be a Villanova Wildcat Ball Boy or Girl at a men's basketball game.

The three-week auction begins at the start of basketball season, right before Christmas. V Club officials guarantee all items will arrive by Christmas, which Rigsby says adds interest as people are able to bid on gifts for fans and alumni alike.

Villanova's sports teams are able to gain additional benefit from the auction by providing items of their own, with the net proceeds from these items going to their respective programs. For example, Rigsby says, the baseball team raised $30,000 for its program that way during the last auction.

Rigsby works with sports technology company Sound Enterprises (Norcross, GA), which handles the online aspect of the auction. The V Club pays Sound Enterprises 10 percent of auction proceeds and a 4-percent credit card fee, leaving 86 percent of funds raised to go directly to help support athletes and sports programs.

Like any auction, Rigsby says, the event is not without stress as organizers wonder what the results will be and whether all the work will be worth it. But after 10 years, he says, "We're at a point where we have resolved a lot of the issues and securing items is really more of a renewal process now than cold calling. Plus, we have a lot wider reach online than we would ever have at an event."

Source: Whitey Rigsby, Director, The V Club, Villanova University, Villanova, PA.
E-mail: whitey.rigsby@villanova.edu

Five Steps to a Successful Online Auction

The 10-year-old online auction for The V Club of Villanova University (Villanova, PA) has a strong history of success, raising $80,000 to $100,000 each of the last five years. Whitey Rigsby, V Club director, shares some of what he and his colleagues have learned over the last 10 years to help make an online auction successful.

1. **Find the right company.** It may take a few tries before you find the best match for you. Rigsby says they worked with two or three other companies before finding their best partner in Sound Enterprises.

2. **Network, network, network.** This is the key to one-of-a-kind auction items and repeat donations.

3. **Timing is everything.** Plan your event at a time when you can piggyback on hype or tie into other events. The V Club auction runs between Thanksgiving and Christmas, at the start of the men's basketball season. Fans are pumped up about the new season and people are looking for Christmas gifts.

4. **Be specific.** For vacation home and timeshare items, clarify with the donor when the winner can use the prize. Make sure those dates are listed on the auction site and any supporting documentation. When notifying the winner, make sure to reiterate the dates the prize is available for use.

5. **Do it all at once.** Rigsby says some organizations have open-ended auctions, consistently offering one or two items all year long. "Limiting it to a certain time period allows momentum to build and creates a following. People can count on when the auction is going to be and they start to look forward to it."

Online Auction Companies Can Boost Success

A number of companies are devoted to helping nonprofits succeed at online auctions. Here are a few to check out as you search for the best match for your organization:

- Sound Enterprises — www.soundenterprises.net
- Bidding for Good — www.biddingforgood.com
- Idonatetocharity.org — www.idonatetocharity.org
- Charityfolks.com — www.charityfolks.com
- Charitybuzz — www.charitybuzz.com

The Impact of Facebook and Twitter on Event Planning

Facebook or Twitter? The question of where to commit limited event-promotion resources became a little clearer with a report from event-planning service Eventbrite (San Francisco, CA; www.eventbrite.com).

The study, entitled Social Commerce: A Closer Look at the Numbers, put hard numbers on an often nebulous area of marketing. It placed the revenue generated by a Facebook "like" at $1.34 and a Twitter tweet at $.80.

Does this mean Facebook is a better promotional tool than Twitter? Ultimately, it does, says Director of Marketing Tamara Mendelsohn, citing two main reasons.

"First, connections are stronger on Facebook because they more closely mirror real-life relationships," she says. "Because Facebook involves people you know in real life, if a friend invites you to attend an event, the credibility of that referral is very high. Twitter often centers on national figures or celebrities, and though you might be curious what events those people are attending, you're less likely to actually attend them yourself."

The second difference, she says, is proximity. Facebook friends are more likely to live in your geographic area, raising the likelihood you will attend events they share.

Facebook offers several advantages, but Mendelsohn says the preferences of constituents should always come first. She notes that some organizations might find Twitter to be the superior method of communication, and points out that the far-reaching nature of Twitter lends itself to raising name recognition and awareness.

Studies on social commerce make for interesting reading, but Mendelsohn says such research, especially when associated with specific numbers and dollar amounts, can have very tangible effects on event planners' work. "If you can quantify the impact of social media — documenting how many people are sharing your event through Twitter or measuring how much revenue is being driven by Facebook — you can use that information to make your business case stronger," she says. "It can help with everything from strategic planning to resource allocation."

The Eventbrite report can be found at: http://blog.eventbrite.com/social-commerce-2.

Source: Tamara Mendelsohn, Director of Marketing, Eventbrite, Inc., San Francisco, CA. E-mail: Tamara@eventbrite.com

A Closer Look at the Numbers

The social commerce study conducted by Eventbrite (San Francisco, CA) contains several other nuggets of interest to event planners:

The Point of Interaction

- "Over the last six months, 40 percent of sharing through Facebook occurred on the event page (pre-purchase) vs. 60 percent of sharing which occurred on the order confirmation page (post-purchase). This tells us that the motivation to share is higher once the purchase is made and the attendee is committed."

- "Not only is the motivation to share post-purchase higher, that share is more meaningful ... A post-purchase share on Facebook drives 20 percent more ticket sales per share than a pre-purchase one."

The Channel of Sharing

- "Over the last six months, sharing activity on Facebook equaled almost four times the amount of sharing on Twitter. We attribute this to Facebook's reach ... and the fact that connections on Facebook more closely mirror real-world, personal relationships."

- "The disparity between Facebook and Twitter is also highlighted in the raw dollars generated per share. ... A Facebook "like" drives an average $1.34 in ticket sales, compared with a tweet that drives an average $.80."

Sharing by Event Type

- "Networking events had the highest share rate, followed by business events and conferences and seminars."

- "When we look at dollars per share by type of event, though, we find that shares are most valuable for music events and concerts, at over $12 per share. Next most valuable are shares for fundraisers ($11), social events and mixers ($7), and food/wine events ($5.50). ... So, while people are more likely to share business-related events, sharing information about social events drives the most sales."

Website Helps Nonprofits Succeed at Event Promotion

Eventbrite, one of the leading online event promotion companies, is reaching out to help nonprofits through the Eventbrite for Causes program.

The program strives to help nonprofits further their missions through successful events. Participating organizations have the opportunity to use Eventbrite to publish, promote and sell tickets to their events through the site using a special nonprofit rate. The rate is a per-ticket transaction fee of 2 percent of the ticket price plus $0.99 per ticket sold, which organizations can choose to pay themselves or pass on to their attendees.

For more information visit www.eventbrite.com/npo?ref=blog.

Virtual Walkers Extend Event Reach

Your fundraising walk is a big day. But it's just one day — and what about the hundreds of people who can't make it on that day? Or the ones, who could have made the date, but live too far away?

Virtual walkers are the answer, says Jennifer Matrazzo, associate executive director of Prevent Child Abuse New York (PCANY), Albany, NY. "Virtual walkers can still raise money towards the event without having to actually be there," Matrazzo says. "The idea is really just another way to expand the scope of our walk and give people a reason to become fundraisers for us."

Walkers register through the organization's website as virtual walkers. Like actual walkers, virtual walkers are directed to firstgiving.com, where they can create their own personalized fundraising page. PCANY pays Firstgiving an annual fee for providing this service.

Another outside vendor, Democracy in Action (Washington, D.C.), handles event registration, e-mail marketing, contact management and other Web-based functions for a monthly fee, based on the number of supporters in PCANY's database.

"We were already using both of these vendors for other events," says Matrazzo, "so there wasn't any additional cost associated with adding virtual walkers. We were just finding a new use for technology and services we already had at our disposal."

This is the organization's first year of offering walkers this option. Matrazzo says the response so far has been light, but she is hopeful. "As we continue to promote the concept through e-mail and other channels, I'm hoping it will pick up. As with most events, the challenge is getting people involved. I'm hoping that a combination of persistence and creativity will result in an increased response."

Source: Jennifer Matrazzo, Associate Executive Director, Prevent Child Abuse New York, Albany, NY.
E-mail: jmatrazzo@preventchildabuseny.org

Online Fundraising Essentials, Second Edition.
Edited by Scott C. Stevenson.
© 2012 Stevenson, Inc. Published 2012 by Stevenson, Inc.

Online Fundraising Essentials — 2nd Edition

THE WEB'S ROLE IN MAJOR GIFTS

Although you may never receive a five- or six-figure gift via your website — though it does happen from time to time — you can use this medium to establish, cultivate and steward relationships with major gift donors and prospects. You can recognize top donors and feature stories about the impact of major gifts on those you serve. You can educate the public about your endowment and share major gift opportunities. And you can share achievements that stregthen your credibility as a cause worthy of donors' investments.

Use Your Website to Help Cultivate Major Gifts

Although your website in and of itself may not generate major gifts, what's on it can help nurture those gifts.

Here are examples of what may cultivate financially capable prospects who visit your website:

- Defining naming gift opportunities and listing them.
- Listing and describing existing named endowment funds.
- Doing feature articles on realized planned gifts and the donors.
- Touting your nonprofit's most significant achievements.
- Presenting facts, figures and history of your endowment.
- Displaying your board members' names and positions.
- Delineating planned gift opportunities.
- Sharing facts and figures that speak to your organization's fiscal strength.
- Citing the impact of past major gifts on your nonprofit and those you serve.
- Sharing information and updates regarding your capital campaign and/or strategic plan.
- Displaying contact information of advancement personnel.
- Placing your case statement online.
- Describing the benefits of upper-end gift clubs and inviting participation.
- Including donor recognition measures.

Website Offers Tools, Tips To Secure Major Gifts

Everyone can use more tools to help secure major gifts, and the Corporation for Public Broadcasting (Washington, D.C.) has put together quite an arsenal at www.majorgivingnow.org.

The site was created to help the nonprofit public television organization and its affiliate stations address an ongoing issue — how to successfully secure major gifts. Assisting in the website development were some development heavy hitters and numerous public broadcasting stations across the country.

The website is devoted to giving CEOs, development professionals and leadership volunteers the tools to begin and improve major gift fundraising. While it is designed for public broadcasting stations, most of the information and tools are broad-based enough to help your organization, too.

Your Website Should Evoke Visitors' Curiosities

Your website is at its most effective when it inspires visitors — especially major gift prospects — to want to learn more about your organization. For that reason, websites should not simply divulge every fact about an institution, but rather lead the visitor to ask questions that only a phone call or e-mail to your organization could answer.

Come Up With Q & A About Your Endowment

Whether you're meeting one-on-one with a potential endowment donor or educating visitors to your website, it's helpful to have a series of questions and answers about your endowment to educating and cultivating the public.

Here are some general endowment questions for which you might want to provide answers:

1. What is the size of your endowment?
2. Who oversees investments?
3. What percentage of endowment earnings is used for programs each year and how much is returned to the corpus?
4. Can I restrict a gift to endowment?
5. Is there a minimum-sized gift you will accept for the endowment?
6. Can I restrict my endowment gift to a particular project or fund?
7. Do you prefer outright or planned gifts when they are directed to your endowment?
8. Is it possible to establish a named endowment fund? How does that work?
9. What types of restricted funds presently make up your endowment?
10. How much do I have to have in an endowment fund before you begin to use its annual interest?

Four-star Assessment Boosts College's Efforts

Calvin College (Grand Rapids, MI) recently received a special honor from the independent charity evaluator, Charity Navigator (Mahwah, NJ): four stars.

That's Charity Navigator's highest ranking for a 501 (c) 3 organization — a big deal to be sure, but Phil de Haan, Calvin's director of communications and marketing, says the ranking is really just a bonus, not the reason they do what they do.

"We've never run our fundraising operation at Calvin with an eye toward the rankings. We've always felt that our fundraising operation at Calvin College is effective and efficient," de Haan says.

Supporting that belief is the fact that organizers of Calvin's most recent capital campaign actually beat their $150 million goal by $5 million.

How did Calvin garner the top ranking from Charity Navigator?

"There was not a lot that Calvin had to do," de Haan says. "Charity Navigator does all of the legwork in terms of finding the data they need to make an informed and complete evaluation. On our end our main responsibility was simply doing things right — filing IRS Form 990 and working hard to be responsible and trustworthy stewards of the financial resources people entrust to us."

That work includes helping people understand why supporting the college is important and that Calvin officials will be good stewards of those gifts, de Haan says, adding, "Something like the Charity Navigator ranking is one more thing that gives people confidence in Calvin."

Source: Phil de Haan, Director, Communications and Marketing, Calvin College, Grand Rapids, MI. E-mail: dehp@calvin.edu

Ripple Effect Waves in Support for Capital Campaign

Phil de Haan, director of communications and marketing, Calvin College (Grand Rapids, MI), says ongoing efforts to develop meaningful and lasting relationships with donors were critical in the success of their recent $155 million capital campaign.

One tool that helped build loyalty with prospective donors was telling stories of alumni impacting the world, and thus, living out the mission of the college, which in part states that Calvin students "offer their hearts and lives to do God's work in God's world."

In sharing the stories, de Haan says they were able to say that a gift to Calvin was not just helping the college and its students, but many other projects and organizations worldwide. That ripple-effect argument was a positive message during the campaign that resonated with donors and helped contribute to the campaign's overwhelming success.

Could Charity Navigator Give Your Fundraising a Boost?

Could your organization benefit from an evaluation by Charity Navigator (Mahwah, NJ)?

Founded in 2001, Charity Navigator offers an objective, numbers-based rating system to assess the financial health of more than 5,000 of America's best-known charities. Named as one of TIME Magazine's 50 coolest websites, www.charitynavigator.com — the website for Charity Navigator — helps guide philanthropic giving and, in its own words, help nonprofits "by shining lights on truly effective organizations."

The company considers these guidelines before evaluating any organization:

1. **Tax status.** Charities must have tax-exempt status under Section 501(c)3 of the Internal Revenue Service Code and file Form 990.

2. **Source of revenue.** Public support must be $500,000-plus in the most recent fiscal year.

3. **Length of operation.** Organizations must have filed four years of 990 forms to be considered.

4. **Location.** Scope of nonprofit's work can be international, but operations must be located in the United States and organization must be registered with the IRS.

5. **Program types.** According to its website, Charity Navigator is not currently accepting hospitals, hospital foundations, universities, community foundations, PBS stations, land trusts or preserves.

To have your organization evaluated by Charity Navigator, register at www.charitynavigator.org and complete the online request form. Registering gives access to advanced benchmarking tools.

Allow Viral Campaigns to Run Their Course

In today's tech-savvy world, word travels fast. And when your supporters start texting and tweeting about your major event or capital campaign, then their friends forward that news to their friends, the campaign has gone viral.

"Giving in to serendipity is part of the entire concept of going viral," says Nonprofit Consultant Ken Goldstein of Goldstein Consulting (Los Gatos, CA). "If a campaign is driven from top-down, with a command and control attitude that was approved in endless closed-door meetings, then by definition it's not viral, no matter how popular or successful it may be."

To be truly viral, Goldstein says, a campaign must be person-to-person sharing out of true interest, "not carefully orchestrated, scheduled and monitored organization-to-masses distribution." Unfortunately, he says this troubles many professional fundraisers and boards of directors because the very things that make something viral also prevent it from being put in a budget with any accuracy.

While going viral in the virtual world may be a new trend, the concept of such groundswell support is not. As long as there have been nonprofits, there have been people-driven efforts to support them, from bake sales to asking for donations in lieu of birthday gifts. "The difference in the social media age is scale," Goldstein says. "Instead of supporters bringing in a few hundred dollars from the couple dozen people they are in physical contact with, the message is quickly forwarded electronically to friends of friends of friends, and the results can be huge."

All nonprofits should be prepared for a fundraising effort, publicity campaign or other communications element to go viral, Goldstein says. To do so, he advises:

- Truly engage friends and followers with social media. Be on Facebook (www.facebook.com) and Twitter (www.twitter.com) with regularly posted updates, including photos of your events and good deeds. Don't just post and run. Listen to what others are saying, and reply swiftly. Remember, social media is not a broadcast medium; it's a conversation platform.

Two Viral Campaign Nevers

You may think you know what to do to be prepared for a viral campaign, but do you know what not to do? Nonprofit Consultant Ken Goldstein, Goldstein Consulting (Los Gatos, CA) cites two key elements to keep in mind to make your viral campaign a success:

1. **Never force it.** "Your online audience is message-savvy and knows the difference between a true viral message and being marketed to."

2. **Never correct your supporters.** "If you have somebody sending donors your way, don't yell at them for using the old tag line, messing with the schedule for your other events or not sending it out to the right people. Only if the message is so off-base or incorrect that you'll end up in legal trouble should you ever get in their way."

- Have a large, easy-to-find Donate Now button on every page of your website.

- Make your website accessible and easy to read (and donate) from mobile devices. "This includes phones, iPads and whatever is invented next week," says Goldstein.

- Think phones. If your message goes viral, bringing people to your website, and it's not maximized to be read on a phone or have a call to action front and center, he says, "You've just blown your opportunity."

Finally, the nonprofit consultant says, the social media-driven concept of viral marketing is so new that there are no experts, "only practitioners and slightly more experienced practitioners. So learn from your peers. See what other, similar organizations are doing and evaluate their success."

One of the most effective ways to do so is through Twitter, he says. "Start following other nonprofits and fundraisers, using the 'Follow Friday' Twitter tradition, where users recommend their favorite tweeters. If somebody you respect is recommending somebody else, follow them, broaden your circle and pay attention."

Source: Ken Goldstein, Goldstein Consulting.
E-mail: ken@goldstein.net

Online Campaign Launch Reaches Broad Audience

Live video, online chat rooms, pictures, games and prizes. It was all part of a first-of-its-kind online event announcing the launch of the Bold. Brilliant. Binghamton Campaign for Binghamton University, State University of New York (Binghamton, NY).

"We were looking for something different for our campaign launch," says Rebecca Benner, campaign director, "something that would make a big splash and would reach a broad audience, but would be cost effective."

On April 22, 2010, organizers unveiled the campaign's public phase by launching a website made specifically for the event.

"We contracted with an event consultant who had done many extravagant launches and inaugurations, but was exploring ways to utilize technology to create event experience in a virtual world," says Benner.

Once logged on, viewers could watch a live, streamed announcement of the campaign goal; clever videos featuring dozens of university faculty, staff, students and donors; photos of the campus; Binghamton-themed games and a video contest where anyone could submit their 60-second Bold and Brilliant video for a $1,000 prize.

"The event had to be very interactive to hold the attention of the attendees. We included very little text and a lot of video content, games and the opportunity to communicate with peers and favorite professors," says Benner.

A welcome video provided an introduction to the various components available while a Twitter feed and chat rooms

hosted by Binghamton faculty, students and alumni kept many entertained. "The most popular feature of the event was the party rooms or chat rooms that focused on either a featured faculty member or affinity groups. The various affinity groups certainly helped spread the word to enhance participation at the event," says Benner.

The campaign's goal is $95 million, with $42 million supporting student excellence, $45 million for faculty and academic programs and $8 million to fund current operations. At the launch event, Benner says, campaign officials announced they had already raised $82.9 million during the quiet phase of the campaign, which began in 2005. "That left us with just over $12 million to raise during the public phase. The event itself was not a fundraiser, but we certainly had a Make a Gift link on the event website which resulted in a dozen or so gifts during the event," Benner says.

The campaign, which runs through June 2012, has raised some $87 million to date.

While Benner calls the online campaign launch a success, she cites several factors she would change next time: "It would have been great to have had more chat rooms available based on interests/affinities. We also wish we would have scripted the live broadcast a bit more. It was a little too hard to follow for those viewing it remotely."

Source: Rebecca Benner, Campaign Director, Binghamton University, State University of New York, Binghamton, NY. E-mail: rbenner@binghamton.edu

Is Facebook the Right Place for Your Campaign Ad?

Are you wondering if a Facebook ad would be a worthwhile investment for your campaign?

Susan Pyron, assistant vice president, annual giving, alumni and parent relations, Gettysburg College (Gettysburg, PA), says the effort was worthwhile for its Cly-Del Challenge, helping raise awareness of the campaign and more than $630,000 for the college.

Working with the Web communications and marketing office, Pyron's department took out two ads on Facebook (www.facebook.com) at a cost of less than $100 each. Both ads targeted people in the United States who graduated from

the college, then split between those age 22-32 and 33-64 to determine if ads were more effective with younger, more recent alumni. The results indicated no difference between the age groups, she notes.

College staff used an appeal code to track gifts, and Pyron says that while the number of gifts received was small, the effort was worthwhile because of the exposure, reaching close to 500,000 people with less than $200.

Source: Susan Pyron, Assistant Vice President, Annual Giving, Alumni and Parent Relations, Gettysburg College, Gettysburg, PA. E-mail: spyron@gettysburg.edu

Maximizing Online Giving

On Give to the Max Day held each November, officials with GiveMN (Saint Paul, MN) ask Minnesota residents to dig deep to raise funds for favorite nonprofits online.

During the 2010 event, some 42,596 donors logged on to GiveMN.org to give $10,041,021 in 24 hours, reflecting donations as well as matching grants and prizes awarded, and bringing the total GiveMN has helped nonprofits raise in the event's two-year history to $27 million.

During its 2009 event, more than 38,000 donors logged on to the www.givemn.org website, grossing more than $14 million for 3,434 Minnesota nonprofit organizations. The 2010 event included the goal to engage 40,000 people to give to their favorite Minnesota charities.

"The 2009 event was an auspicious start for GiveMN, which was created to help Minnesotans discover, support and directly engage with organizations that match their giving goals," says Dana Nelson, executive director of GiveMN.

Nelson offers the following tips for driving your online fundraising efforts:

✓ **Get personal.** Answer the question: What inspires you about the cause and the organization? Make your appeal and story personal and highlight your motivations for asking for funds. Sharing your passion for the cause will inspire donors to contribute, too.

✓ **Be visual.** Nothing helps more than a vivid photograph or a compelling video about your cause, featuring interviews and insights about the impact that a donor will have.

✓ **Give it a deadline.** Whether it's a matching grant that expires or a goal to raise a certain amount of money in a given time frame, give donors a reason to give now.

✓ **Make it a contest.** Encourage donors to start a contest to see who can raise the most for your organization. They can grow mustaches, have a Wii tournament or do anything else they enjoy — all to support your cause!

✓ **Show specifics.** Show exactly how you will use a $10, $20 or $100 gift. Describe how giving more will result in greater impact.

Source: Dana Nelson, Executive Director, GiveMN.org, Saint Paul, MN. E-mail: dana@givemn.org.

Display a Virtual Donor Wall on Your Website

You may have a lobby donor wall that depicts the names of last year's annual contributors, or perhaps you have a walkway with bricks displaying the names of donors. Why not use that same approach and create a visually appealing virtual wall on your website?

Whether it's a donor wall or a giving tree that lists donors, get creative and come up with a way to display names of donors on your website. It's yet another way to give donors the recognition they deserve and can be easily viewed by donors whose geographic distance prevents them from visiting your facility or campus.

Examples of Virtual Donor Walls

Wabash College (Crawfordsville, IN) — www.wabash.edu/alumni/terrace.cfm

Adventist Health / Central Valley Network — http://adventisthealthcv.netreturns.biz/newsreleases/Article_Detail.aspx?id=ee369683-794e-4a42-a631-a3fac1a90bd3

South Texas College of Law (Houston, TX) — http://www.stcl.edu/alumni/donor-wall/index.html

Mayo Clinic (Rochester, MN) — http://www.mayoclinic.org

Find a Place for Annual Reports in the Digital Age

According to the Blue Avocado (www.blueavocado.org), a San Francisco, CA-based online magazine for community nonprofits, people do only four things with nonprofit annual reports: read the letter, check to see if they're listed (if they're a donor), read the captions on the photos and look at the financials to see how big you are and if you had a surplus or a deficit.

In spite of this and the digitization of many traditional publications, Project Manager Susan Sanow says there is still a place for this nonprofit staple. "My spin on annual reports is that they provide an essential stopping point. Digital age or not, you need to stop, measure and report out regarding how the organization is doing."

Writing the annual report is also writing the history of the organization, says Sanow. "I did annual reports for another organization for 15 years. All of those staff members and board members are gone. Without a history, who knows what happened and when? Only the annual reports can really tell that information. I also think that if people approach their 'transparency obligations' along with annual report activities, they can work well in tandem."

Source: Susan Sanow, Project Manager, Blue Avocado, San Francisco, CA. E-mail: susan@blueavocado.org

Video Lets Donors Meet the People Their Gifts Help

As a donor, what would it mean to you to be able to directly see the faces of the people you have helped?

Zach Pretzer, associate director, Oberlin Alumni Fund, Oberlin College (Oberlin, OH) says a video created by Oberlin to honor and thank the college's generous scholarship donors does just that.

The nine-minute video is featured on the college's website (www.oberlin.edu/giving/scholarshipvideo/). It offers testimonials from those who have received scholarships to Oberlin as well as those who have made donations in support of Oberlin's scholarship programs.

Scholarship recipients also share reasons specific to their own situations why scholarship gifts are so important.

Sophisticated and creative editing adds the final polish to the piece.

Pretzer says the video is just one example of the way Oberlin makes stewardship a priority. "We excel in strengthening relationships with donors by honoring those who invest in Oberlin and help serve the needs of our donors through scholarship reporting, recognition and events."

Source: Zachary Pretzer, Associate Director, Oberlin Alumni Fund, Oberlin College, Oberlin, OH. E-mail: zach.pretzer@oberlin.edu

Online Video Brings Attention to Donor's Spectacular Gift

An eight-minute video highlighting a donor's gift of a sculpture garden to North Central Michigan College (Petoskey, MI) has brought attention to how donors can make a difference on campus.

The video, donated by Jack Harris, shares the story of Harris Gardens. College officials share it by posting it on the foundation's website (http://www.ncmich.edu/harris/harris.html) and using it in presentations to community service clubs and campus groups.

"(The video) allows us to talk about a donor's impact on our campus," says Sean Pollion, executive director of the college's foundation. "It has also been a great way to strengthen our relationship with the donor, who has already requested 100 copies of the video to share with his friends, family and colleagues."

College officials created the video in-house over two months at a cost of about $3,000, says Charlie MacInnis,

director of public relations. In-house writer, Kathryn Bardins, prepared the script and interviewed the college president, Harris, and artists who created the sculptures. She also worked with the video crew to capture the art installations.

"The sculpture garden is a spectacular sight," says Pollion. "It has transformed the campus. We have our major donors walk through it when visiting campus. It has put us on the map as an organization that can get philanthropic support at this level."

Another benefit to the video is its timelessness, says Pollion: "There is no expiration date. Five to 10 years from now it will continue to tell the story of this donor's gift, why he became involved and his affiliation with the college."

Sources: Sean Pollion, Executive Director, Charlie MacInnis, Director of Public Relations, North Central Michigan College Foundation, Petoskey, MI. E-mail: spollion@ncmich.edu or cmacinnis@ncmich.edu

Feature Monthly Gift Profiles on Your Website

Whether you provide your constituents with a regular e-newsletter or simply encourage them to visit your website, consider featuring a monthly or quarterly online story about a recent major gift. Not only does this provide an additional way of recognizing top donors, it plants seeds in the minds of those who read about the gifts' positive impact. It opens others up to the possibilities of philanthropy.

In addition to covering both the donor and the impact of the donor's gift, your feature might include links to additional information pertaining to some aspect of your story.

Online Fundraising Essentials, Second Edition.
Edited by Scott C. Stevenson.
© 2012 Stevenson, Inc. Published 2012 by Stevenson, Inc.

Online Fundraising Essentials — 2nd Edition

HOW OTHERS ARE RAISING AWARENESS AND FUNDS ONLINE

The fastest and most efficient way of developing a program is often learning from the example of others. Check out this sampling of ways in which other nonprofit organizations are using their websites and online communications to raise gifts and strengthen relationships with donors and would-be donors.

Raise Money, Social Awareness With Green Campaign

Dovetail your fundraising efforts with an issue that is high on the social consciousness, and you're likely to drum up positive attention along with donations.

As part of Southern Polytechnic State University's (Marietta, GA) commitment to reduce its carbon footprint and incorporate sustainable practices and initiatives into its strategic goals, organizers decided to eliminate all paper promotional materials for this year's faculty and staff campaign and promote mostly online.

The university's Go Green Faculty and Staff Campaign saved 1,260 pieces of paper and 846 envelopes, says Pierrette Maillet, coordinator of annual giving.

"The green approach was definitely successful," Maillet says. "Aside from the resource and energy savings, many faculty and staff gave us positive feedback on the green focus of the campaign."

The 2009 campaign participation rate was 55 percent (211 individual donations), compared to 67 percent the previous year (248 individual donations), but Maillet attributes the drop to the economy and not to the green initiative. SPSU has 438 full-time faculty and staff.

To lead the green effort in 2009, the university's advancement department asked Jim Cooper and Julie Newell, two champions of environmental sustainability on campus, to serve as campaign co-chairs. Cooper is executive director for sustainability initiatives and Newell is an academic department chair and organizer of a very successful campus Earth Day celebration involving the Girl Scouts.

Using an online format for promotion eliminated the need to print packets filled with a promotional postcard, a page listing accounts, a page listing giving incentives, a pledge card, a return envelope and labels for each, says Maillet.

All of those materials went online except for the pledge card, she says, which was accessed online but had to be printed out as a PDF because the university's auditors required the foundation to include the donor's signature on each pledge form, especially since most pledges are made through payroll deduction. To further the go green impact of the campaign, donors were encouraged to send the pledge form through interoffice mail in a recycled envelope.

To help get the word out about the fundraising campaign without using paper products, some 35 campus-wide volunteers were encouraged to talk with their constituent groups about the campaign. In doing so, they were asked to point the constituents to the Go Green campaign's Web address to learn more or to make their pledge entirely online.

"Through this campaign, the advancement office sent a message about our commitment to going green," says Maillet. "Although it would have been easier to conduct the campaign like we had always done it, we wanted to do our small part to advance sustainable practices. We received no complaints, only compliments and kudos!"

Source: Pierrette Maillet, Coordinator of Annual Giving, Southern Polytechnic State University, Marietta, GA. E-mail: pmaillet@spsu.edu

Fly-through Tour Brings the Future to Prospective Donors

"The video is magical."

H. Ken DeDominicis, Vice President for Institutional Advancement, University of St. Thomas (Houston, TX) is talking about the donor impact of the online fly-through tour of the university's planned Center for Science & Health Professions. "The fly-through tour was actually prepared by an architectural firm at their cost to pitch for the job of designing the proposed center."

At the time of the request for proposals, the economic recession prompted the selected architectural firms to make very impressive and extravagant proposals. Many of the architects did extensive visual and media presentations. Therefore, the university had no cost involved in securing this outstanding video.

An example of the magic DeDominicis is talking about is the receipt of a check for $2 million to endow a chair for the nursing program within three working days from the time the presentation was made to a foundation board to receipt of the check. DeDominicis says, "We have also presented it to select individuals with the capacity to make major naming

opportunity gifts, including naming of the building. To date we are in discussion with gifts of that magnitude thanks to the impact of the video."

The tour is being used for targeted personal presentations and group presentations, as well as broad distribution in social media and direct e-mail distribution. The university is using a microtag in their promotional magazine, and on postcards to targeted audiences to maximize exposure. The tag has also been used to show the video on smartphones in places like restaurants over lunch or dinner.

The target audience for the tour is very broad, says DeDominicis. "Our intent is to target the specific major donors as well as promote the center broadly among all audiences, including parents and students who might be attracted to attend the University of St. Thomas."

Source: H. Ken DeDominicis, Vice President for Institutional Advancement, University of St. Thomas, Houston, TX. E-mail: ken@stthom.edu

Online Tribute Pages Help Donors Raise Further Funds

"If you had the chance to save the life of someone you love, wouldn't you take it?"

That is the question asked on the philanthropy portion of The Scripps Research Institute (La Jolla, CA) website, and officials there are hoping that people will answer it with one of their newest philanthropic tools, the Scripps Research Tribute.

The research tributes (www.scripps.edu/tribute/home/), which were started a few years ago with the assistance of Sankynet (www.sankynet.com) in New York, NY, began as a way to bring a more personal approach to funding for biomedical research, says Scripps Research's Philanthropy Associate Elliot Wolf.

Individuals can create a tribute either in honor or in memory of someone special in their life, by uploading a photo, writing a personal note and choosing a designation for all gifts made to that tribute. "For example," says Wolf, "If I were to create a tribute in memory of a grandparent who had Alzheimer's, I could choose that all gifts made to that tribute be directed to Alzheimer's research."

A unique URL is given to each tribute and visitors to the page can leave a comment or donation. The page can also be forwarded to their friends, family and colleagues to make gifts to the tribute.

Wolf says even without any real advertising or marketing to speak of, there have already been about 30 tributes set up, raising anywhere between $10 and $10,000, depending on how the tribute creator shares it with friends and family.

Wolf says the tributes are a great way to engage a memorial-tribute donor and also gives them a tool to reach out to their friends.

"Biomedical research can seem so cold and academic. This is a way to make it warm and personal, while honoring the legacy of a loved one through research that may one day result in cures. It also allows people to have an outlet for simply sharing comments, as well as making gifts."

Wolf says they are just starting to market the tributes, with several marketing efforts in the works right now, and are excited to see how much response they get moving forward.

Source: Elliot Wolf, Philanthropy Associate – Marketing & Donor Research, The Scripps Research Institute, La Jolla, CA. E-mail: elliotw@scripps.edu

---

Accept Quick and Easy Online Payments

Drive donations to your nonprofit by utilizing online payment programs. Consider adding one of these online payment programs to your site:

- **Auctionpay** — (www.greatergiving.com/all-products/auctionpay.aspx) Auctionpay offers the option of having onsite payment and card readers at auctions, galas or golf tournaments allowing winning bidders to pay and go.
- **Brown Paper Tickets** — (www.brownpapertickets.com) This site allows you to create an event, buy preprinted tickets to an event and process payments.
- **Click & Pledge** — (www.clickandpledge.com) This program offers a trio of fundraising options which include collecting donations online, donor management and building an online community.

Build Awareness, Branding With Interactive Online Game

An animated online game is helping raise awareness for the Feral Cat Trap-Neuter-Return Program of the Austin Humane Society (www.austinhumanesociety.org) (AHS), Austin, TX.

A year ago, officials launched Trapcat (www.austinhumanesociety.org/resources/trapcat), an interactive, animated game on its website in which site visitors attempt to trap cats that pop up around familiar Austin landmarks at increasing speed by clicking on the cats when they appear.

"We feel (Trapcat) really captures what we are trying to accomplish in terms of engaging the community using a fun yet educational tool," says Lisa Starr, public relations manager.

Suzanne Kyba is vice president of brand strategy at Door Number 3 (www.dn3austin.com; Austin, TX), an advertising, branding and media firm that designed Trapcat exclusively for the AHS.

"We knew that the more we could illustrate AHS' personality on the website and give people opportunities to interact with AHS, the better," Kyba says. "We wanted to develop ways that the audience could spend time with the brand."

Trapcat is played in stages, with feral factoids popping up between stages. The average amount of time a user spends on the Trapcat page is two minutes, Kyba says, and since its launch, the page has generated over 3,000 unique visitors — without any marketing dollars to promote it.

"The feral cat program is one that many people don't understand and can feel apprehensive about, so we developed this game as a solution that provided a fun way to engage with AHS, educate and help to demystify the program," says Kyba. "We made sure to represent feral cat trapping in a lighthearted way that still communicated the powerful benefits of spaying and neutering stray animals."

Starr says that Trapcat "creates a sense of community and encourages volunteerism and participation in our Feral Cat Trap-Neuter-Return program."

Sources: Suzanne Kyba, Vice President, Brand Strategy, Door Number 3, Austin, TX. E-mail: skyba@dn2austin.com
Lisa Starr, Public Relations Manager, Austin Humane Society, Austin, TX. E-mail: lstarr@austinhumanesociety.org.

HOW OTHERS ARE RAISING AWARENESS AND FUNDS ONLINE

Video Contest Helps Ambassadors Define School's Voice

Considering offering or revamping a video contest for your organization? Realize the important role participants play.

"Most successful social media campaigns are driven by key constituents," says Becca Ramspott, public information specialist, Frostburg State University (Frostburg, MD). That certainly was the case for the school's Frostburg: Take 5 video contest. "The contest allowed our students and alums to tell us how we're doing and join our conversation about how we define our institution."

School officials launched Frostburg: Take 5 in 2007 with a general call for videos from students and alumni. Videos had to be five minutes or less. The result? Videos that provided valuable additions to the collective story of why Frostburg is a great place to go to college.

"We got several great videos and learned a lot about how to conduct a successful YouTube contest. It inspired us to return to the idea in fall 2010," Ramspott says.

For 2010, they refined guidelines and added cash prizes. They also required that participants' videos reflect one of three themes: I Chose Frostburg, Frostburg: The "Reel" Deal or My Heart Will Always Belong to Frostburg.

A panel of five judges determined prize winners ($125 to $500). Online voting through the university's YouTube channel determined the People's Choice Award winner. Winners were announced during a special awards ceremony that also included a screening of the winning videos.

The contest is proving to be a real boon for marketing the school, says Ramspott, which was one of the reasons for creating the contest. "We wanted new videos we could use for marketing and admissions purposes, and doing a contest seemed like a great way to get free video content. Through it, we were able to obtain very authentic and creative videos we can use for marketing purposes."

Additionally, she says, "This contest invited our students and alums to really think about their relationship with FSU, and how they perceived FSU in positive and amazing ways. This was an exciting creative experience that really engaged them as storytellers and ambassadors of our institution."

Source: Becca Ramspott, Public Information Specialist: Technology and New Media, Frostburg State University, Frostburg, MD. E-mail: reramspott@frostburg.edu

What a Video Contest Can Do for Your Organization

Public Information Specialist Becca Ramspott, Frostburg State University (Frostburg, MD), says her institution's video contest reaped multiple benefits for everyone involved. Here, she cites four reasons Frostburg is planning to repeat the contest:

- Viral marketing possibilities. Ramspott says a lot of Take 5's promotion and the actual contest itself were conducted on social media. People who saw these videos and liked them could share them with their own friends on Facebook, YouTube, etc.

- Great publicity. Frostburg: Take 5 earned FSU inclusion in a front-page Washington Post article.

- Connections with constituents — new and old. Ramspott says FSU reconnected with new alumni who participated in the contest and created new connections with the judges.

- Inspiring collaborations. Ramspott has formed great collaborations with her colleagues on campus as a result of the contest and other social media projects she's done. "The contest helped me discover people on campus beyond the Communications & Media Relations team who are interested in social media and can provide much-needed resources in technology. I head up a Social Media Group at FSU that includes folks from IT, online education, etc., whom I first met through efforts like Take 5. They have helped me pull off many social media marketing projects, which has been wonderful."

Website Feature Ideas

Online custom calculators can provide an interactive opportunity for anyone who visits your website.

For example, a new website tool on Goodwill Industries International's website calculates the impact a donated item will have in terms of training those the organization serves.

Check it out at: http://donate.goodwill.org.

Online Fundraising Tip

- Do you ever see a feature on some other nonprofit's website that you want to copy but forget to do? To prevent that from happening, start a list of particular features you find on other websites that you want to implement one day. Then you'll be prepared to make those updates at the appropriate time.

HOW OTHERS ARE RAISING AWARENESS AND FUNDS ONLINE

Side-by-side Illustration Moves Donors to Give

Joette Rosato, director, Seton Hall Fund, Seton Hall University (South Orange, NJ), wanted to create a visual to make people really think about what making a donation means: "After working in alumni relations for seven years and moving on to development, I felt there was something missing in the way people think about donating. So I started thinking about the process of education of donors and thought that might be a good route to go."

That feeling, along with results of an alumni attitudinal survey, led Rosato to use an illustration of water glasses bearing logos of Seton Hall and five other Big East schools, each filled to reflect that college's giving rates (shown at left). Seton Hall measured in at 8 percent, the lowest of all the schools.

Rosato and university officials used the visual in many mediums, including print, Web and e-mail. They incorporated the comparisons into the university's spring appeal, as ads on the university's website and used it for a smaller appeal involving the alumni board of directors.

Rosato says the giving statistics surprised many people, and that the illustration had the desired impact.

"Seton Hall alumni, students, parents and friends are a proud group of people, so the pride is there," Rosato says. The challenge in encouraging gifts "is getting them to take

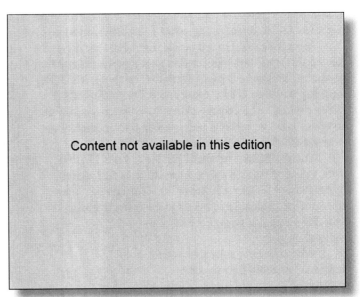

Content not available in this edition

the next step. Many think that the other guy is donating, so why should they? This comparison showed them that, obviously, isn't the case."

Source: Joette Rosato, Director, Seton Hall Fund, Seton Hall University, South Orange, NJ. E-mail: Joette.Rosato@shu.edu

Volusion Offers Free Online Stores for Nonprofits

Volusion (www.volusion.com; Simi Valley, CA) is a for-profit corporation that develops and designs online stores for a wide array of Internet-based businesses. For nonprofit organizations looking to increase their Internet-based revenue, Volusion's Stores to Change the World program provides the same level of software and service options at no cost.

Each month, Volusion awards 10 501(c)3 organizations a Gold-level store for life at no cost.

"This means that nonprofits can sell products online, receive needed donations and multiply awareness of their causes," says Molly Sylestine, a service sales consultant based out of the company's Austin, TX, office. "All they have to do is focus on expanding their mission, while we take care of the rest."

Volusion's Gold stores are considered a tier above the standard service plan because the software package includes an API, a connector to third-party software. Sylvestine explains, "We give the Gold store as the free version for nonprofits, because they may need to connect to accounting software or other integrations."

A nonprofit's Gold store can be used to sell products for the organization's financial benefit, but it can also be used to accept straight donations. Sylestine says that the latter is what

most nonprofits choose to do with their Gold stores. "They have a button that might say, 'Donate Now.'"

In order to qualify for the free Gold store, a nonprofit must be a certified, U.S.-based 501(c)3 organization; its mission statement cannot be politically or religiously focused; and the organization must not discriminate on the basis of race, ethnicity, national origin, religious affiliation, gender, sexual orientation, age, disability, physical appearance, language, educational background or veteran status.

Sylestine notes that a nonprofit "can be affiliated with a religion, like a church food pantry whose mission is to feed the hungry, but the mission can't be religious in nature."

Volusion currently maintains more than 300 free Gold stores for various nonprofits. The company usually receives between 10 to 15 applications per month from nonprofits requesting a store, which means virtually every nonprofit that applies is accepted.

"Really the only way a nonprofit's application would be declined is if it had a mission that didn't match the criteria," says Sylestine.

Source: Molly Sylestine, Service Sales Consultant, Volusion, Austin, TX. E-mail: Molly_Sylestine@volusion.com.

HOW OTHERS ARE RAISING AWARENESS AND FUNDS ONLINE

Social Media Offers New Twist on Old Campaign

The health insurance company CDPHP (Albany, NY) has long been a supporter of the Regional Food Bank of Northeastern New York (Latham, NY).

One way CDPHP staff show support for the food bank is with the CDPHP Holiday Appeal, in which the company donates $5,000, and then pledges to match donations of $100 or more from other companies up to an additional $5,000.

In honor of the tenth anniversary of the appeal and in recognition of the increasing importance of social media in promotions and fundraising, CDPHP partners decided to add a new twist: matching donations of $100 or more up to $5,000, and donating $5 for every new "like" on the food bank's Facebook account up to an additional $5,000.

The switch helped raise more than $5,000 in addition to the $10,000 donation from CDPHP, says Mark Quandt, food bank executive director. Quandt adds that the food bank's Facebook friend numbers are growing fairly quickly, too, largely due to the CDPHP appeal.

The campaign has been widely promoted through local media coverage, area newspaper ads, billboard exposure, mail solicitations of CDPHP's vendors and prior food bank donors, and an e-newsletter sent to 2,500 food bank supporters.

Source: Mark Quandt, Executive Director, Regional Food Bank of Northeastern New York, Latham, NY.
E-mail: markq@regionalfoodbank.net

Websites Fundraise for You

A number of websites allow nonprofits to generate funds by having supporters go through the websites to make online purchases, search the Web and perform other online tasks.

Two such websites are GoodSearch (www.goodsearch.com) and GoodShop (www.goodshop.com). The sister websites send proceeds to nonprofit organizations every time a user conducts a search or makes an online shopping purchase.

GoodSearch is a Yahoo!-powered search engine that donates a penny per user search to the charity of that user's choice. Organizations must first enroll by clicking on the Add a New Charity button on GoodSearch's homepage and completing a brief application. Approval generally takes just a couple days, says JJ Ramberg, co-founder of GoodSearch, which currently works with more than 86,000 nonprofits and receives applications for about 100 more per day. Donations come from GoodSearch's advertisers.

GoodShop.com is an online shopping mall where merchants donate a percentage of online purchases to shoppers' designated charities. More than 700 stores participate, including Amazon, BestBuy, eBay and Travelocity. Charities must likewise enroll to begin receiving revenue.

Users must first go to GoodShop.com, then click through to their desired merchant's website. Or, they can do a one-time download of the GoodSearch/GoodShop toolbar.

The Mommies Network (Monroe, NC), a nonprofit dedicated to helping mothers find support and friendship in their communities, has raised nearly $5,000 since July 2007 through GoodSearch and GoodShop, says Heather Fortune, president and founder. She says the key to raising funds through these online search tools is "regularly reminding our members about GoodSearch and Goodshop and continuing to encourage them to use it.

"Every time we make a new announcement, we see a surge in our numbers," says Fortune. "It is important to keep it front and center, in front of our members."

Sources: Heather Fortune, President and Founder, The Mommies Network, Monroe, NC. E-mail: heather@themommiesnetwork.org
JJ Ramberg, Co-founder, GoodSearch, LLC, Los Angeles, CA.
E-mail: jj.ramberg@goodsearch.com

Flash-y Greeting Touches Constituents

Looking for a unique way to reach out to your constituents? Think Flash — a Flash movie that is. Susan Goetschius, Director of Communications, Alfred University (Alfred, NY) said they created one to use as a holiday electronic greeting (www.youtube.com/alfreduniv#p/u/57/5eM1rMWr1TM) that was sent to all alumni for whom they had a valid e-mail address, roughly 10,000 people, starting in December 2005 and have done so ever since.

The Alumni Relations, Annual Giving and Communications offices were involved in selecting images that related to experiences that span generations of alumni (e.g., the snow in Alfred; Hot Dog Day, which is a common experience for those who graduated in the past 35 years; and St. Patrick's Day for older alumni). Once the images were chosen, the school's Web team created the Flash movie.

The piece was designed to engender positive feelings among alumni, which it definitely did, says Goetschius. "Of the 10,000 people who received it, about 2,000 opened it. The feedback was positive, with most comments focused on warm feelings and Alfred University memories."

Source: Susan Goetschius, Director of Communications, Alfred University, Alfred, NY. E-mail: goetschius@alfred.edu

Online Fundraising Essentials, Second Edition.
Edited by Scott C. Stevenson.
© 2012 Stevenson, Inc. Published 2012 by Stevenson, Inc.

TIPS FOR EVALUATING ONLINE EFFECTIVENESS

To improve your online fundraising success and build your website's value as a donor-friendly destination, it's important to keep testing and evaluating everything you have been doing: social media measures, e-campaigns and communications and more. That ongoing evaluation will point out what's working, what should be eliminated and what might be improved.

Social Media — Can You Measure Its Worth?

Social media is making unforeseen inroads into communications. But what is that traffic worth, in terms of communications, for a nonprofit?

To determine that, we turned to Menachem Wecker, social media expert with The George Washington University (GW), Washington, D.C., and chair of the 2011 Council for Advancement and Support of Education (CASE) Annual Conference for Media Relations Professionals. Wacker is a writer and editor at *George Washington Today,* GW's official online news source, a co-founder of the Association for Social Media and Higher Education at GW, and an active Twitter, LinkedIn and Facebook user and blogger.

Wecker shares what he believes nonprofits should consider when dipping their toes in the pool of social media.

What is the science of measuring cost versus return on social media?

"I would be concerned about any claim that there is a science of measuring the cost versus return on social media. There is certainly a cost, but the return is not often embedded in analytics. Some organizations trumpet 1,000 fans on Facebook as an achievement worthy of a press release. I think a large number of Twitter followers or Facebook fans or blog comments are not necessarily a function of successful use of the medium. The more important question is how well the organization is using social media to integrate into a larger community. That's often a gradual process.

"That said, there is a general rule of thumb that I advise: It is vital to be authentic in social media. Those who have handles on a variety of social media platforms, including Facebook and Twitter, can notoriously sniff out overly congratulatory and institutional language. Social media can be used to lend personality and individuality to your brand, but it can also, when wielded improperly, bore your constituents to tears."

What are the best resources nonprofits can use to help them evaluate their efforts?

"I think nonprofits can learn the most about how well they are doing in their communications strategy by asking their constituents. There are a variety of online tools to track your success, helping you to contextualize your digital footprint, but none of that is as important as talking to real people. If you are communicating properly, you are going to hear positive feedback from the people on the other end of your communications."

> *"Nonprofits can learn the most about how well they are doing in their communications strategy by asking their constituents. There are a variety of online tools to track your success, helping you to contextualize your digital footprint, but none of that is as important as talking to real people."*

What can nonprofits on shoestring budgets do to make the most of their public relations efforts?

"There are a lot of things that don't require a lot of money, if any at all, like staying on top of your institution's Wikipedia page to creating a Twitter handle and a Facebook page. Blogs can be set up for virtually no cost. What is becoming increasingly difficult to buy (even if you have an unlimited budget) are colleagues who have the courage and the curiosity to jump into social networks and explore. If you've got people willing to take that plunge, you would be surprised how far a shoestring budget can stretch."

When does it make sense to turn to an outside professional to help with your efforts?

"I think only if you aren't equipped to do it yourself, or if that professional is going to work in concert with your own efforts. New social media tools help curate direct communications. The more links there are in a broken telephone game, the more the message is lost. I'd encourage nonprofits to communicate directly with their constituents. If you only have time to communicate occasionally with your community, then you might consider bringing help in, but not in place of that direct communication."

Source: Menachem Wecker, The George Washington University, External Relations, Washington, D.C.
E-mail: mwecker@gwise.gwu.edu

Analyze Social Media Efforts to Measure Return On Investment

You begin by placing an important announcement on your organization's website. Next, you tweet a link to the announcement asking your Twitter followers to check it out. A few days later, you post a synopsis of the announcement on your blog, including a link to the original Web page. You might even send another tweet announcing the blog post.

And because you integrated Twitter into your LinkedIn and Facebook pages, additional fans, friends and contacts receive the news through those outlets.

Such cross-fertilization makes for good communication strategy while providing a body of concrete metrics to gauge social media efforts' effectiveness, says David Sieg, vice president of strategic marketing, YourMembership.com, Inc. (St. Petersburg, FL).

Sieg says the following areas are particularly suited to measurement:

✓ **Inbound clicks.** The amount of traffic social media communications are driving to your website is an important measure of overall impact, says Sieg. How many users are clicking through to your site from your blog? From your Twitter tweets? From your Facebook page? Measure this information and use it.

✓ **Industry links.** Links are the mark of online relevance, and the number of industry groups and prominent bloggers who link to your website suggests the regard in which your organization (or at least its published content) is held, says Sieg.

✓ **Audience.** Whether friends or fans, subscribers or followers, your loyal audience members are another easily tabulated metric. But Sieg cautions that readership is only a first step, and that user-initiated interaction — filling out a contact page, downloading a contact form, reposting your article — should be the primary goal.

✓ **Search engine optimization.** Your organization's organic page rank (the place it appears on a search engine's page of unpaid search results) is a matter of great importance, says Sieg. Not only does it reflect the number of people viewing your content and linking to your posts, it determines how easily potential members will be able to find your online presence. Never ignore a rising or falling page rank.

✓ **Website analytics.** Google Analytics (www.google.com/analytics), the gold standard of free website analysis, can determine many of the previous metrics including clicks, links and referring sites. Website usage patterns

---

Steps to Building a Workable Social Media Strategy

While social media is new territory for many organizations, its underlying strategy is not as foreign as some might imagine, says David Sieg, vice president of strategic marketing for YourMembership.com, Inc. (St. Petersburg, FL).

"It's important to start a social media strategy by defining a concrete goal — a membership level, dollar figure, etc. — that is quantifiable and has a relatively short-term end date, maybe a year to 18 months," Sieg says.

The next step, he says, is devising objectives, both social and traditional, that further this goal. "If your goal is achieving X number of members by 2012, you might say you will send Y direct mail pieces, launch a social media marketing campaign via Twitter and LinkedIn, and commit Z dollars to advertising."

Finally, he says, devise operational tactics supporting each objective.

This planning process must include development of a defined content strategy.

"Firing random thoughts out across Twitter will not get the job done," says Sieg. "You need a consistent voice, a consistent message, and a consistency of communication across many kinds of media. An annual schedule of communication, detailing by quarter or month what will be sent out to whom by what portal, is an invaluable part of any social media initiative."

---

revealed by online analytics — how long users view any particular page, what pages users leave your website from, what percentage of users landing on a contact page actually fill out the form — also give clues about user preferences and behavior.

Finally, Sieg says, do not ignore conventional metrics. "Is your membership growing? Is your revenue increasing? Are your services being utilized? These are areas on which social media should be having an impact and, therefore, should constitute another form of measurement."

Source: David Sieg, Vice President, Strategic Marketing, YourMembership.com, Inc., St. Petersburg, FL. E-mail: dsieg@yourmembership.com

Online Surveys Improve Website Efficiency

Unlike websites of for-profit companies or online retailers, nonprofits' websites usually don't sell a tangible product. But the intangibles they sell — a cause, a call to action, a service, as well as a user's overall online experience — are just as valuable. More and more, nonprofits are taking a cue from the for-profit sector and working to enhance that website experience with online surveys.

Since 2008, the website (www.nmh.org) for Northwestern Memorial Hospital (NMH), Chicago, IL, has included a pop-up survey (one that appears in a small separate window) designed and implemented by an outside company, ForeSee Results of Ann Arbor, MI.

"We use (the survey) as a means to improve the experience of the people going to the site by enhancing offerings, navigation and features," says Holli Salls, NMH vice president of communications. "It is about providing the kind of information people are looking for. Our goal is to have our patients find what they need when they need it, or to help provide education and information to others who might be seeking help."

Since the survey went live, 36,559 visitors (out of 18.9 million total site visitors) have been asked at random to take the survey, NMH's marketing department reports. Of those, 6,484 people (18 percent) elected to complete the survey.

Since implementing the survey, Salls says, NMH

officials have made several website improvements, including improving navigation and linkage; adding a comprehensive physician-finder section; adding an auto-complete function to site searches; factoring keywords, misspellings and best bets into those searches; and adding social media bugs to the homepage. ForeSee officials provide numerous measurements for analyzing survey data, such as a usability audit that pinpoints areas for a website's improvement, plus regular satisfaction index reviews.

Steve Wierdak, NMH's program manager for market research, says they chose ForeSee because, "it is a leader in the Web satisfaction survey space, as well as the fact that their methodology utilizes the American Customer Satisfaction Index, developed by the National Quality Research Center at the University of Michigan, which has been the leading national indicator of customer satisfaction with goods and services in the U.S. economy since 1994, and goes in tandem with NMH's focus on quality."

Wierdak says they are working on enabling website visitors to opt to take the survey upon exiting from the website so they may complete their website visit without interruption.

Sources: Holli Salls, Vice President of Communications; Steve Wierdak, Program Manager, Market Research; Northwestern Memorial Hospital, Chicago, IL. E-mail: hsalls@nmh.org or swierdak@nmh.org.

Survey Programs Offer Basics Free

Wondering what changes your members would like to see in your organization? Find out by using a survey program on a consistent basis. Surveying your members is a fast, efficient way to incorporate changes within your membership and a simple way to test the pulse of your members.

Here are details on some of the leading survey programs:

- **Web Survey Master** — www.websurveymaster.com — offers survey and quiz tools for all professionals. Its free basic service allows for a maximum of three surveys and 100 responses per month. Professional survey levels begin at $19.95.

- **Survey Monkey** — www.surveymonkey.com — a popular surveying service, assists in market research. It is user-friendly and offers a basic essentials plan at no cost as well as a premium plan starting at $17.

- **Zoomerang** — www.zoomerang.com — allows users to create unlimited surveys or polls and send them by way of e-mail, Facebook or Twitter. This service offers 12 different options, and its free basic service allows for 12 questions and 100 responses with real-time results. Zoomerang also offers advanced service levels for an annual fee starting at $199 per year.

Evaluate Your Website's 'Table of Contents'

Continually refine your website, as you do your other outreach materials, to best capture the interest of your donors and potential donors.

Increasing numbers of nonprofit websites have several pages devoted to gifts or giving. When you click and arrive at the primary giving page, you find a table of contents that categorizes topics related to giving.

Put some thought into that index or table of contents to make it as easy as possible for website visitors to navigate your site. It's equally important that you prioritize what should be included in that listing, knowing there are many headings from which you can choose.

Here is a sampling of headings (in no particular order) from which you might choose in creating your gift section's table of contents:

❑ Alumni	❑ Annual Gifts	❑ Annual Report
❑ Capital Campaign	❑ Case Statement	❑ Class Giving
❑ Gift Levels, Clubs	❑ How to Give	❑ Matching Gifts
❑ Contact Us	❑ Corporate/Foundation Gifts	
❑ Endowment	❑ Examples of Generosity	
❑ Events	❑ Frequently Asked Questions	
❑ Planned Gifts	❑ Naming Opportunities	

Leverage Charity Navigator Rating to Your Advantage

Michael Nameche, director of development, Chicago Coalition for the Homeless (Chicago, IL) has a story about the growing importance of the independent charity evaluator, Charity Navigator (Glen Rock, NJ): "My mom was planning to donate to a charity and decided to look them up on Charity Navigator. When she found out they received only two stars, she called me up and told me she had reconsidered her donation."

His mother's reaction is not unique, says Nameche. Several of his donors have told him they only give to charities receiving Charity Navigator's highest, four-star rating.

Founded in 2001, Charity Navigator (www.charitynavigator.org) has become the nation's largest evaluator of charitable organizations.

Using information from organizations' IRS Form 990s, the service rates financial health according to organizational efficiency and organizational capacity. From a range of individual metrics, a single numerical score is calculated and a rating of zero to four stars is determined.

A four-star rating is like a badge of honor that can be used to enhance fundraising efforts, says Nameche. "If someone is looking at your organization and thinking about donating, that four-star logo makes them feel like they are making the right choice."

While the coalition uses the Charity Navigator logo on Web pages, e-mail blasts and direct mail pieces, the rating system behind it is not without shortcomings, says Nameche. "It takes a financial snapshot at the fiscal year end, which is not always an accurate representation of overall health," he says. "990s are one window into an organization but they don't give the whole picture. They don't say anything about the results behind those dollars-per-person-served calculations."

Nameche's advice regarding Charity Navigator is simple: Use your rating as best as you can, but make sure you also explain how your organization is changing lives.

Source: Michael Nameche, Director of Development, Chicago Coalition for the Homeless, Chicago, IL. E-mail: michael@chicagohomeless.org

Tool Takes Narrative Approach To Charity Evaluation

The independent charity evaluator, Charity Navigator (Glen Rock, NJ), is a powerful rating service, but many persons have pointed out that its data-driven methodology is inherently limited.

To share your organization's story as widely as its numbers, Michael Nameche, director of development, Chicago Coalition for the Homeless (Chicago, IL), suggests turning to social media-based services like GreatNonprofits (http://greatnonprofits.org) and GuideStar (www2.guidestar.org).

"These sites allow individual users to not only grade nonprofits, but to write narrative accounts of their experience with them," creating a more comprehensive and well-rounded assessment, he says.

Development officials can easily add their organization to these sites and begin building positive word of mouth by asking volunteers, members and clients to post their experiences online.

Three Tools to Evaluate Giving Catalogs

Jasmine Hoffman, manager of public relations in institutional advancement, University of Pittsburgh (Pittsburgh, PA) says their online giving catalog has been a hit with alumni, prospective donors and development officers alike. How did they know that would be the case when they were developing the catalog? They did thorough research and utilize Web analytics. Hoffman offers the following tips to make sure similar tools work effectively for you:

1. **Do your research first.** Hoffman says focus groups and online surveys told them that many of their donors visit the university's website to explore giving opportunities before completing an online gift or contacting the development office. This led them to believe the catalog would be a natural extension of that need for research and information.

2. **Understand how your donors think.** A comprehensive card sort analysis helped them understand how donors organize giving opportunities and terms on the website. Hoffman says, "The card sort analysis helped us identify the categories and terminology to use in the giving catalog. We wanted the giving catalog to be donor-centric so we thought it was appropriate to organize it according to the responses from the card sort analysis."

3. **Use the technology available.** Hoffman says Web analytics have allowed them to see that the students' category is the most successful area within the giving catalog and that most Web visitors are navigating to that section of the catalog first. Analytics have also allowed them to know how many unique page views the site has received and how many people leave the website after viewing only one page. All of this information allows them to tweak the catalog to make it more user friendly.

Source: Jasmine Hoffman, Manager of Public Relations in Institutional Advancement, University of Pittsburgh, Pittsburgh, PA.

Lightning Source UK Ltd.
Milton Keynes UK
UKOW012319110713

213588UK00006BA/268/P